SHREVEPORT CHRONICLES

SHREVEPORT CHRONICLES

Profiles from Louisiana's Port City

ERIC J. BROCK

THE
History
PRESS

Published by The History Press
Charleston, SC 29403
www.historypress.net

First published 2009

Manufactured in the United States

ISBN 978.1.59629.761.6

Library of Congress CIP data applied for.

Notice: The information in this book is true and complete to the best of our knowledge. It is offered without guarantee on the part of the author or The History Press. The author and The History Press disclaim all liability in connection with the use of this book.

For Shannon Glasheen,
My Colleague, Dearest Friend and Wife

CONTENTS

ACKNOWLEDGEMENTS

For their kind assistance in making possible the original columns on which this book is based, I wish to acknowledge the staff of the Louisiana State University in Shreveport Noel Memorial Library Department of Archives and Special Collections, the staff of the Shreve Memorial Library Special Collections and Genealogy Departments and the original publishers of my columns, the *Shreveport Journal* and the *Forum News Weekly*, each of which gave me the opportunity to publish within its pages while retaining copyright and ownership of my writings. I also wish to thank those descendants of several of the personalities featured in this book who shared information with me regarding their ancestors. Lastly, but far from least, I wish to thank my wife, Shannon Glasheen, formerly a curator with the Louisiana State Museum in New Orleans, whose assistance in doing research, proofreading and editing has proved invaluable many times.

The Jacobs family of Shreveport, circa 1890. Edward and Palestine Jacobs (center row, third and fourth from left) with their children, children's spouses and grandchildren in front of their Travis Street mansion. *Author's collection.*

INTRODUCTION

The biography of a city is really the collective biography of that city's people. In the pages that follow, an attempt is made to tell the story of Shreveport's historical pageant through the lives of a cross section of that pageant's cast of characters. Obviously, there is not space enough for such an undertaking to be comprehensive. Far, far more personalities associated with the city's history are left off these pages than are included in them. However, the selections given attempt to represent an accurate portrait of the men and women from many diverse walks of life and many diverse ethnic and religious backgrounds who have contributed to the city's development and, indeed, have created the city's very character.

Not everyone whose biography is treated in this book was necessarily a citizen of Shreveport, though most were. Some came here from elsewhere or sojourned here during a period of their life and the city's life. All had a lasting impact on Shreveport, however.

Here are heroes and scoundrels, businessmen and religious leaders, artists and soldiers, pioneers and planters, physicians and lawyers and, well, just a number of stories that are ironic, bizarre or simply curious.

No comprehensive list of notable Shreveporters exists, but there are many. The city has produced more notable figures in music, sports, politics, theatre, the visual arts, business and other endeavors than many a city twice its size. The biographies in this book are not necessarily those of its "greats," the many notables who have so frequently been discussed in print that they are familiar to all. Rather, this book seeks to tell the story of the city through people both ordinary and extraordinary who contributed to Shreveport's growth and development—or in some cases merely to its legends and lore—through their unique and often accidental roles in the unfolding historical pageant that began in 1836 and continues even yet. The biographical vignettes included herein were originally written as articles for the author's popular historical columns "The Presence of the Past," which ran on the "Journalpage" editorial page of the *Shreveport Times* newspaper between 1992 and 2000, and its successor, "A Look Back," which ran in the *Forum News Magazine* from 2000 through 2008. The Journalpage was the last vestige of the old *Shreveport Journal*, Shreveport's long-lived evening newspaper that closed in 1991 but, through a joint operating agreement with the *Times*, remained in publication as a daily editorial page within the surviving paper. When the joint operating agreement ran out on the first day of January 2000, the author carried his column to the *Forum*. All told, the column ran weekly for sixteen years and gained a wide following during that time.

The selection of articles that forms the basis for this book draws from those written for both publications, though these have been substantially edited and revised to reflect data discovered after the original publication of the articles and to generally bring them up to date.

FOUNDERS AND PIONEERS

J.B. Pickett, Co-founder of Shreveport

One of the most influential figures in the early development of Shreveport and the Shreveport area was a man named James Belton Pickett, who, along with Captain Henry Miller Shreve and six others, established the Shreve Town Company, the corporate entity that founded Shreveport in 1836. Today he is memorialized only by a small and neglected street in the Crosstown-Bluegoose area southwest of downtown, but his influence, and that of his heirs, played a significant role in the early growth of Shreveport and Caddo and Bossier Parishes.

James Belton Pickett was born in Chester County, South Carolina, in October 1803. His family were planters and he, too, made planting his career. In 1833, at the age of thirty, he married the fifteen-year-old daughter of another wealthy Chester County planter family, Paulina de Graffenried. The couple had three children: John, born in 1834; Sarah (known as Sallie), born in 1837; and James Jr., born in 1840.

In 1835, Pickett's friend, another South Carolinian named Thomas Taylor Williamson, urged Pickett to invest in a land speculation venture in Louisiana. A new town was being laid out on the newly navigable Red River and Williamson, a partner in the company establishing the settlement, convinced Pickett that the investment would change his life; it did just that.

While the Shreve Town Company was being formed, the Pickett family remained in South Carolina. Meanwhile, Pickett himself was acquiring vast holdings of land throughout the newly opened northwest Louisiana

Sallie Pickett Cummings (left) and Paulina Pickett, daughter and wife of James Belton Pickett. *Painting by François Bernard, 1854. Courtesy of Westin Adams, Columbia, South Carolina.*

region, including a 640-acre tract in what is now Sabine Parish, a large amount of property in southern Arkansas and considerable holdings along Red River in what was then part of Claiborne Parish but now is Bossier Parish.

In 1841, the family moved to Shreveport, then a frontier town. What a dramatic change it must have been from their genteel lifestyle in South Carolina. First residing in town, they soon established themselves on a plantation called Cottage Grove across the river and to the north of what is now Benton.

In the spring of 1842, Pickett traveled back to South Carolina to check on his business and planting interests there. On his return trip to Shreveport, he fell ill at Henderson, Kentucky, and there died on June 4 at the age of thirty-eight. His body was sent on to Shreveport and was buried on his property in Bossier Parish. Eventually, the family cemetery in which he was interred became the nucleus of what is now the historic Cottage Grove Cemetery, located on Highway 160 just west of Highway 3.

Paulina took on the operation of the family's plantations herself. According to the 1850 census, her landholdings in Bossier Parish alone were worth $321,000 (about $10 million in today's terms) and she owned 201 slaves. In 1843, she married another area planter named James Blair Gilmer, a widower originally from Alabama. Gilmer owned numerous plantations in Louisiana, Alabama and Cuba as well as land in east Texas. Their marriage created what may have been the largest combined fortune in north Louisiana at that time.

In 1854, Sallie Pickett, then sixteen, married a prosperous New Orleans cotton factor named Robert Campbell Cummings. Cummings, then forty-one, knew the family well through dealings both with Paulina and James Gilmer. Sadly, the marriage was not to last long, for six months after the wedding, Sallie fell ill with cholera and died at the home of her mother and stepfather, the Orchard plantation, in north Bossier Parish.

The grief-stricken family erected a massive white marble monument to Sallie next to her father's grave. Its amazing epitaph covers the entire monument on all sides and can still be seen today. A portrait of Sallie and her mother once hung in the Spring Street Historical Museum downtown but was taken back by the son of the original lender, who sold it through a New Orleans auction house in the 1990s. For several years, it hung above the reception desk of the Iberville Suites Hotel in New Orleans, a subsidiary of the adjacent Ritz-Carlton. After Hurricane Katrina in 2005, the painting was sold to a descendant of James Belton Pickett's sister, Charlotte, and today it resides in Columbia, South Carolina.

Painted in New Orleans in 1854, a copy of this life-sized double portrait was made by the same artist, François Bernard, in 1858 for Sallie's widowed husband. That portrait today hangs in the Williams Research Center of the Historic New Orleans Collection. Robert Campbell Cummings lived to the age of eighty-one but never remarried. Long residing both in New Orleans and at Shady Grove plantation in Bossier Parish (site of the modern-day neighborhood of the same name), he carried Sallie's handkerchief with him until his dying day. Late in his life, Campbell resided at LaChute and Campo Bello plantations in south Caddo Parish. He died at the latter in 1892. Four years later, he was reburied beside his beloved Sallie.

In 1856, while embroiled in divorce proceedings from Paulina—a rarity in that day—James Gilmer died of yellow fever while in Havana; he was forty-two. His body was returned to the United States, where he was buried at Oakwood Cemetery in Montgomery, Alabama, beside his first wife, Eliza Lewis, who had died in 1839 at age twenty-two.

Paulina moved from the Orchard to another of her plantations, Cash Point, before finally settling in a town house in Shreveport at the northeast corner of Milam and Edwards Streets. In 1880, she brought a suit claiming ownership of the Shreveport riverfront. That litigation would be tied up in court for years and never satisfactorily settled. That same year her son, James Jr., died and was buried at Oakland Cemetery downtown, along with the family of his wife, Katie, daughter of Judge Roland Jones and granddaughter of North Carolina governor Montfort Stokes; Katie died in 1886.

Paulina died at her Shreveport home on June 6, 1899, at the age of eighty-one. Her eldest son, John, who married Carrie Doles, daughter of a Bossier Parish planter family, served as state treasurer of Louisiana during the waning years of the nineteenth century. He died in 1900 and was buried at Cottage Grove, next to his mother, father and sister Sallie. In time, his widow and two of their children would come to rest there also. No Picketts have been buried at Cottage Grove since 1929, but a number of descendants still live in the Shreveport–Bossier City area. James Belton Pickett's most visible legacy, however, lives on in the continued growth and development of Shreveport, the city he co-founded as the result of an investment that truly did change his life.

Lawrence P. Crain, Early and Influential Mayor

One of the early important figures in Shreveport's development was a man named Lawrence Pike Crain. Unfortunately, little is remembered today about this man who served as one of the city's youngest mayors, helped establish the first municipal cemetery here and more than once refused to run for Congress because he would have opposed friends.

Lal Crain, as he was known to friends and associates, was an exceptional figure. In 1841, he was all of twenty-three years old when he was elected to the town board of trustees (today's city council). Reelected in 1842, he continued to serve on that board almost perpetually until his death. In 1846 and 1847, Crain served the city as mayor, the sixth man to hold that position. It is interesting to note that even as mayor, Crain continued to hold his council seat, the rules then being quite different from today.

Lawrence Crain was born in Fauquier County, Virginia (in a part now in Loudoun County), on January 25, 1818, but was brought up in Rapides Parish, Louisiana. In early 1848, he married Rachel Adelaide

Lawrence Pike Crain. *Courtesy of LSUS Noel Memorial Library Archives.*

Stokes, daughter of Montfort Stokes, a Revolutionary War veteran, former governor of North Carolina and former Indian agent for the Arkansas Territory. Rachel's sister, Ann Neville Stokes, in 1844 married Roland Jones, a member of the Louisiana House of Representatives and later a U.S. congressman. All eventually made their homes in Shreveport, as did another sister, Rebecca, wife of John J. Kline, co-owner of Phelps & Kline, an early and important local insurance agency.

The Crains were the parents of four sons, John, Robert, Montfort and Lawrence Sidney. Lawrence Sidney Crain penned and privately published his *Reminiscences* in 1882. Though numerous references to this book exist, no actual copies of it seem to have survived. Lawrence Sidney's wife, Mary Henry Ford, was the daughter of the Reverend J. Franklin Ford, third pastor of the First Presbyterian Church, where Lawrence P. Crain was a charter member and one of the first church trustees.

In 1847, Lawrence P. Crain helped to secure a ten-acre tract of land on what was then the town's western edge for use as a city cemetery. This land was purchased from Mary Cane and her father, Dr. Sam Bennett, for an undisclosed price. Mrs. Cane was the first white woman to settle in Shreveport, coming here from New Hampshire with her trader-trapper first husband, his brother and her father even before the original incorporation of the village of Shreve Town. Although an earlier burial ground existed on Fannin Street, the land secured for the city by Mayor Crain and his successor, Robert Nathaniel Wood, is today Shreveport's oldest cemetery, Oakland.

In 1849, Crain helped edit the first codification of Shreveport's city ordinances, compiled by William Wallace Wood and the town's board of trustees. Crain, still a trustee, was also U.S. district attorney for eastern Louisiana by that time and frequently traveled between Shreveport, Monroe and New Orleans. The family home was then located at the southeast corner of Milam and Market Streets (present site of the Crystal Oil Building), with Crain's law office located directly across the street at the northeast corner. The house, built in 1846, was a two-story affair built in the style prevalent in New Orleans in that day, with cast-iron galleries across the front and a courtyard behind. Perhaps Crain had admired New Orleanian homes during his many trips to the Crescent City and decided to create his own in a similar fashion. In any case, it was one of Shreveport's very few brick houses when it was constructed. After Crain's death, the house was sold by his widow to the Citizens Bank of Louisiana, which remodeled it into the bank's Shreveport branch; it stood until 1903.

On January 25, 1859, Lawrence P. Crain celebrated his forty-first birthday in New Orleans, where he was staying at the St. Louis Hotel, then the Crescent City's finest. The St. Louis, built in 1838 and rebuilt following a fire in 1841, then charged $2.50 and up per night at a time when decent lodgings could be found for only pennies. The hotel was the center of life, both social and commercial, in the New Orleans of the 1850s and it was there, on January 28, 1859, a Friday night, that Lawrence Pike Crain breathed his last. Long a sufferer of tuberculosis, he unexpectedly succumbed to that disease.

Crain's body was brought back to Shreveport, where he was buried at Oakland Cemetery. He rests there yet, beneath a large marble slab at the cemetery's eastern edge. Next to him lie his wife, their four sons, one daughter-in-law and a granddaughter, Ethel Lewis Crain, who died in 1966 at age eighty-three. Rachel's sisters' families, the Joneses and the Klines, rest at Oakland also. In 1904, Newton Crain Blanchard, Lawrence P. Crain's nephew (the son of his sister, Frances Amelia Crain Blanchard), became governor of Louisiana, having already served several terms in both the U.S. House and Senate between 1881 and 1897.

In 1859, having initially moved from the Milam Street house to a residence at Lake and Spring Streets, Rachel Adelaide Crain lived her last years at an address on Southern Avenue between Jacobs Street and Margaret Place. As for the building where Lawrence P. Crain died, the St. Louis Hotel, it became the Louisiana Statehouse following the Civil War and later was remodeled into a grand hotel once again (the Hotel Royal). In September 1915, a hurricane severely damaged it, and in 1917, it was demolished except for a row of arches along Chartres Street that can still be seen today. They are part of the Omni Royal Orleans Hotel, which now occupies the site.

Robert N. Wood: Shreveport Mayor and Filibuster

Robert Nathaniel Wood, the seventh mayor of Shreveport, is an enigmatic figure. He was not here long and thus his name has not been burned into the city's collective memory, as have the names of many of his contemporary pioneers. Yet Wood was an ambitious man, a politician and an adventurer, and his story is a fascinating and romantic one.

Robert N. Wood was born in Virginia in 1818 and was raised in Maryland. In his youth, he went to Texas, then a wild and undeveloped country. The Republic of Texas, newly liberated from Mexico, beckoned young Wood and he heeded its call. While there he read law, becoming an attorney, though engaging in farming as well. Even before Texas was admitted to the union, Wood returned to the United States, settling first in Alabama and then in Mississippi and practicing law in both places.

While in Mississippi, Wood, then still in his twenties, married a girl named Frances Nixon, born in Mississippi and not yet sixteen at the time of her wedding. In 1843, the couple moved to Louisiana, settling in the relatively new town of Shreveport. Shreveport, founded in 1836, was still on the frontier and was as far west as one could go before crossing the international frontier into Texas. The young and turbulent river town attracted the adventurous spirit of Wood, who immediately threw himself into the political and social life of the place.

For several years, from 1845 or 1846 until 1849, the Woods resided in a one-story frame house at the southwest corner of Travis and McNeill Streets, a house evidently built by Wood. In November 1848, Wood bought a lot at the northeast corner of Fannin and Marshall Streets and contracted with builder LeGrand DeForest Nash for the construction of a spacious, four-room center hall house with a wide front porch, a detached kitchen and smokehouse and a garden surrounded by a high cedar fence. In December, he sold the house at Travis and McNeill to Judge Edward R. Olcott for $3,150 (around $150,000 in today's real estate dollars). The house Olcott bought from Wood was later home to Edward Jacobs, another city pioneer, who in the 1880s demolished it, replacing it with a massive Victorian mansion that stood until it, in turn, was replaced by the present downtown YMCA, completed in 1925.

The Woods' new home, not finished until after they had moved in, was to be their residence for less than a year. On April 6, 1850, Wood and his wife (who had a half-interest in the house, which was not the case with their previous property—perhaps she had inherited money of her own in the interim and this helped pay for the grander place) sold their newly finished home for $3,500 to Dr. William N. Head, who was murdered by highwaymen outside of town a few years later. The Wood house was afterward the home of the Winter family for many years and through a succession of later owners suffered numerous alterations, though it remained standing until 1947. The Louisiana Second Circuit Court of Appeals building today occupies the site.

Wood owned other properties locally as well, investing in a number of lots and buildings on speculation. Among these were a lot in the 200 block of Milam Street, north side, and two parcels of real estate in the 500 block of Fannin, south side.

In 1846, Wood ran successfully for city trustee (forerunner to today's city council) and a year later ran successfully for mayor as a member of the Whig Party, serving a one-year term, as was the custom in that era, from May 1847 to April 1848. Losing his office to attorney John Morgan Landrum (later a U.S. congressman) in the reelection, he regained the office from Landrum in May 1849 but in December of that year resigned, having made the decision to join the so-called "forty-niners" and head to California in search of gold. His successor was the Reverend John Bryce, who had come to Shreveport several years earlier as U.S. collector of customs on imports from the Republic of Texas. While here, Bryce assisted in founding the First Baptist Church of Shreveport as well as Summer Grove Baptist Church and pastored both.

California called to Wood like a siren of ancient mythology, and like a siren of ancient mythology it would lead ultimately to his demise. But Robert Nathaniel Wood went to California not only to seek gold from the earth but to seek it in other ways as well. The gold rush also brought a land rush and there was much litigation, a fertile field for an ambitious young attorney. Even beyond that, however, California was on the verge of statehood, a territory just opening up, and so also offered adventure in the process. Besides, Wood had failed to gain a hoped-for nomination to a federal judgeship in Louisiana and had also lost a bid for the position of district attorney in Caddo Parish. Even though he was mayor of Shreveport, it was not enough, and California offered a ground-floor chance at a prestigious position in a new and uncharted land.

So Robert and Frances packed and moved to California in the late spring of 1850, settling in Contra Costa County, across the bay from San Francisco. Wood briefly tried his hand investing in gold mining but quickly returned to the bar and was elected a judge in Contra Costa. As in Shreveport, Wood invested in land and for a time owned agricultural property in what is now the wine country of northern California. Aspiring to a seat on the newly organized California State Supreme Court, he was foiled in his ambition when the winds of political change shifted away from the Whig Party, which dissolved in California, as elsewhere. He switched his affiliation to the American, or "Know Nothing," Party, which briefly held power in California in the mid-1850s. However, that party disappeared almost overnight over the slavery issue and whether California, with its rich and vast agricultural potential, should be a slave or free state, and with it went the careers of a number of ambitious politicians, including Wood. Wood did, however, serve as an elector for former Whig president Millard Fillmore when he ran unsuccessfully to regain the White House on the American Party ticket in 1856.

As in Louisiana, Wood's hopes for appointments to a district attorneyship and a federal judgeship were dashed, as was his later bid for a seat on the state supreme court. His multiple applications, still on file in the National Archives, attest to his ambition. He even garnered the support of the noted Louisiana statesman Senator Judah Philip Benjamin (who, years later, was to hold three Confederate cabinet posts), and cited Benjamin elsewhere as a reference. Disillusioned politically in California, his sense of adventure and ambition led him to join his good friend Henry Alexander Crabb in a scheme to seize power in Mexico.

Crabb was a filibuster, which in the nineteenth-century meaning was one who engaged in private military invasions of foreign lands, namely Central American and Caribbean lands. Bolstered by the success of New Orleanian William Walker, who in 1856 invaded Nicaragua, overthrew the existing government and set himself up as its dictator, the former California state senator and native Tennesseean Crabb that same year plotted to invade and "colonize" the Mexican state of Sonora. With the support of a number of wealthy Californians and a few prominent Sonorans, including members of his Sonoran wife's family, Crabb, with his friend Robert N. Wood, raised a company of some ninety men. In January 1857, the assemblage gathered arms and supplies in Los Angeles and then headed on foot to the Arizona Territory, crossing the border into Sonora in late March.

The filibustering expedition of Crabb and Wood was not welcome in Mexico, which viewed it as a gang of pirates and mercenaries. The party was advised of this by Mexican authorities before entering Sonora. All warnings ignored, the expedition rode into Mexico, with Crabb taking sixty-nine men to the city of Caborca, leaving "Major" Wood with twenty others to follow shortly after the first wave had taken the city. Unfortunately for Crabb, the majority of Sonorans did not support becoming part of the United States and were waiting for him when he arrived with his men on April 1. Brutal fighting raged for six days before the "filibusteros" surrendered, having been offered terms of peace by the Mexican military commander, Hilario Gabilondo. Once disarmed, however, the filibusteros were herded into a stockade for the night, and the next morning they marched to the edge of town and were gunned down in groups of five. Only one survivor remained to tell the story of how the former senator Crabb was then taken to the city plaza, bound to a post and beheaded, his head placed in a bottle of mescal for preservation as a trophy.

Meanwhile, members of Wood's party, unaware of Crabb's fate, were en route to Caborca when intercepted by the Mexicans. After a fierce fight, they attempted to flee toward the United States but were shot down by Mexican troops, and their bodies were dumped into the same mass grave as the rest of the Crabb party on the outskirts of Caborca. Thus came the seventh mayor of Shreveport to rest in an unmarked grave in a foreign land. He was not quite thirty-nine years of age. In Martinez, California, he left a thirty-year-old widow. Although diplomatic protests called the executions "unmitigated murder," the United States dropped the matter after an inquiry determined that Crabb and Wood had violated Mexican law. Their demise marked the end of American filibustering forays into Mexico.

Eldred Ward: A Tragic Tale

The Summer Grove Cemetery is located at the southeast corner of Mansfield Road and the Industrial Loop. It has long been associated with the Summer Grove Baptist Church, which stood adjacent to it for over a century, yet the cemetery was once the town burial ground for the village of Summer Grove, which occupied a portion of what is now southwest Shreveport.

In the middle of the cemetery, not far from the edge nearest the Loop, is a very old stone. It is a curious monument, broken from its base but still quite dignified and rather poignant off by itself as it is. It was made in St. Louis, according to the maker's mark on its base, and bears a much worn and faded image of a female figure weeping over a gravestone. Its

Gravestone of Eldred Ward, Summer Grove Cemetery, Shreveport. *Photo by author.*

inscription reads: "In Memory of Eldred Ward, Born August 25, 1825, Died October 12, 1859." Although there are a few older stones in the cemetery, Ward's is among the oldest that survive. The stone is curious and intriguing; the story behind it is even more so.

William Eldred Ward was a native of Augusta, Georgia, one of nine children. In 1847, he married a young widow named Mary Eliza Wright. Her first husband, Jacob, had died and left her with two daughters whom Eldred, as her second husband was called by friends (family called him "Willie"), adopted as his own. She and Eldred later had two more children, a son and a daughter.

About 1850, the Wards came to Shreveport. The exact circumstances of their coming here are not entirely clear, though many of Eldred Ward's siblings and other relatives had settled nearby in Texas, mostly in the Carthage and Gilmer areas. In any case, in 1854, Ward purchased a tavern called the One-Mile House. It was located where Texas Avenue crosses Interstate 20 today, but in the mid-nineteenth century it was just outside the city, one mile from the center of town on what was then called the Texas Road. The tavern was also sometimes called the Angle House, since it was located right inside the elbow curve of Texas Avenue.

Ward purchased a great deal of property in the vicinity and became a major landowner of Shreveport in that day. There were problems, however, with the exact boundary of the property on which the One-Mile House Tavern stood. Ward's next-door neighbor, a merchant and druggist named William W. Smith, argued that his survey of the boundaries between their properties placed Ward's tavern slightly on Smith's land. Smith insisted that it be moved or torn down. Ward refused. The feud got progressively more heated until finally, about September 20, 1858, Ward shot Smith twice, killing him. Smith, a charter member of the First Baptist Church and a respected merchant and landowner, had evidently been killed by another prominent man of the young city.

The thirty-three-year-old Ward panicked. He would later claim self-defense, which might be true, but the fact that he ran made things go badly for him. He fled to Ringgold, in Bienville Parish, where he had friends and decided to lay low for a while. Meanwhile, a posse gathered to pursue him. In the midst of all of this, W.W. Smith, cut down at age forty-six, was laid to rest in Oakland Cemetery.

The sheriff's posse caught up with Ward at David Tatum's house in Ringgold. Ward opened fire on the pursuers but was shot in the shoulder and subdued. He was brought back to Shreveport and jailed but overpowered his jailers, killing one of them and injuring the other. Now things were really bad.

Captured again, Ward was tried and sentenced to death. All of this took nearly a year to transpire. The two pursuits of Ward each took time, as did transporting him back to town on each occasion. Then there was all the waiting around for the circuit riding judge to return to Shreveport—state district judges then covered huge areas and sometimes took months between holding court at the same location twice.

Sentencing having been handed down in early October 1859, Ward knew he had to escape once again if he were to preserve his life and his family. So escape he did. Together with two other inmates, Artemis Bennett and Columbus Nottingham, Ward broke out of the parish jail then located at Crockett and Market Streets. Bennett and Nottingham fled in one direction and Ward in another: toward his tavern and his wife and family. He was still suffering from the injuries he had received exactly a year earlier when he was shot in the shoulder. The wound had become infected, evidently, and healed badly. Ward had difficulty using his arm to mount a horse, so he headed toward home on foot.

Although the tavern was only a few blocks distant, Ward never got there. Near the present-day location of the Municipal Auditorium, he was spotted by a sheriff's deputy named James Markham. Armed during the breakout, Ward drew his gun on Markham, but just as he was about to fire, a man named Nat Farris, returning home from a hunting trip, saw the situation and opened fire on Ward, killing him.

Eldred Ward became the center of a divided community. Many saw him as a victim, others as a wicked criminal. In essence he was both—a man who made a terrible mistake and then continued to make even more, driving himself deeper and deeper into tragedy. The greatest tragedy of all is the fact that he was a good man, well-to-do and respected, a family man with a wife not yet thirty-five years old, a newly married stepdaughter, Mary Elizabeth Wright Williams, age seventeen; and three younger children, Faithie Wright (later Wisenor), Cecelia Anne Ward (later Bradley) and Payton Ward.

His friends—and he had many (ironically, many were also friends of Smith, whom Ward had killed in the heat of argument)—buried him at the Summer Grove Cemetery rather than in the same cemetery where Smith lay.

Eliza Ward, the young widow, sent her younger children to live with relatives in Gilmer, Texas. She later went to Texas as well, settling finally in Pittsburg, where at least one of her daughters also ended up. Their son, Payton, continued to have an on-again, off-again connection to Shreveport, shifting residence between Shreveport and Carthage, Texas, several times before he and his wife Ellen both perished in Shreveport's great yellow fever epidemic of 1873; they are buried at Oakland Cemetery. All four children and Eliza retained Eldred's considerable property holdings here into the 1880s; most were liquidated after Eliza's death in 1882.

Eldred Ward's descendants turned out to be upstanding, substantial people, though none remained in Shreveport. Ward had been upstanding and substantial too, but a bad situation turned tragic and tarred him with a reputation as a murderer and desperado in many later accounts of the tragic chain of events that ended his life and those of at least two others. The "official" story in the Ward family was that Eldred was killed during a robbery at his hotel. Unfortunately, the story of his demise was a bit more "wild west" in nature.

In any case, the mortal remains of Eldred Ward today lie alone in the Summer Grove Cemetery, a century and a half and one hundred yards removed from one of the busiest intersections in the city of Shreveport. Buried in a quiet, rural village cemetery ten miles from town, Ward now sleeps obliviously in a densely urbanized area of a city he would never recognize today. Yet his story is part of Shreveport's history, and his gravestone, now broken and lying propped against its base, remains as a monument to folly and hot temper and a profound waste of human life.

And what of the One-Mile House Tavern, the situation of which brought about the conflict in the first place? It was not moved. The boundary dispute ended with the deaths of Smith and Ward, as the heirs were apparently able to come to an amicable agreement. Indeed, the One-Mile House—by then known as the Angle House—was run by Ward's stepdaughter and son-in-law, Faithie and William Wisenor (Wisenor was a Shreveport police officer, incidentally), for many years. Not until after William Wisenor's death, which occurred in 1899, was the old inn demolished.

COLONEL LEON MARKS OF SHREVEPORT

Colonel Leon Dawson Marks was one of the city's heroes during the Civil War. In fact, after the war there were a number of newborn male babies in this area named for him—first name Leon, middle name Marks. Similarly, there was a rash of little Kirby Smiths born locally about this same time, named for the commanding general of the Trans-Mississippi Confederacy, headquartered at Shreveport. Today, one of Shreveport's two camps (chapters) of the Sons of Confederate Veterans is named in Marks's honor as well.

Colonel Marks was originally memorialized at his grave site only by a small white marble marker stating "L.D. Marks, Col., 27 La. Inf." This stone was replaced by a somewhat more fitting monument in 1997, though the original marker remains in place as well. Near where he fell, however, is a more significant monument. Cast by Tiffany Studios of New York in

Monument to Colonel Leon D. Marks near the spot where he was mortally wounded, Vicksburg National Military Park, Vicksburg, Mississippi. *Photo by author.*

1910, only eleven years after the Vicksburg battlefield was dedicated as a national military park, it is a bronze relief portrait of Marks mounted on a granite base, overlooking the location where he was fatally injured during the defense of Vicksburg.

Marks, a Shreveport lawyer and newspaper publisher, was born at Bayou Sara in 1829. His father was German and Jewish and his mother was Christian. He was twenty-nine when, on March 10, 1859, he married Amelia Jordan of Shreveport, a first cousin once removed of Julia Dent Grant, wife of Ulysses S. Grant. At the time, there was no great curiosity in this fact, though soon the irony would reveal itself.

Marks, a veteran of the Mexican War while still in his early twenties, had come to Shreveport in the mid-1850s to practice law. In 1857, he was admitted to the state bar, and that same year he co-founded a weekly newspaper, the *Caddo News*, which he edited. It was a short-lived venture, and he soon decided to stick with law instead of journalism. In March 1859, having married and decided to remain in Shreveport, Marks was admitted to the Shreveport bar.

Soon, however, trouble began to brew on the national front. Southern states pondered secession as it became increasingly evident that the federal government was dominated by northern economic interests hostile to those of the South. Marks was selected to be one of four delegates representing Caddo Parish at the 1860 secession convention (the others were Benjamin L. Hodge, Richard T. Buckner and Dr. Thomas J. Allen), where they voted to dissolve the union between Louisiana and the federal government and authorized the legislature to arm the state militia at once.

In January 1861, Marks helped organize the Shreveport Greys, otherwise known as company H, First Louisiana Infantry, the first infantry company organized at Shreveport. Marks became first sergeant of the Greys, serving in Virginia. Later, he was elected first lieutenant of company F, Twenty-seventh Louisiana Infantry, and in this capacity arrived at Vicksburg, Mississippi.

Quickly rising through the ranks, Marks became a captain, major, lieutenant colonel and finally colonel with the Twenty-seventh Louisiana Infantry, serving variously with companies F, S and I. He was among the first engineers to direct the construction of fortifications and the mounting of guns at Vicksburg. He was considered to be one of the most capable, efficient and valuable officers at Vicksburg, as well as one of the most popular. His service, however, was not to be long-lived.

Vicksburg was the key to the South, since it was the key to the Southern defense of the Mississippi, called "the backbone of the nation." For over a year, the Confederates had defended it against every Union assault, but in late May 1863, the Union struck with all its might and the forty-seven-day-long siege of Vicksburg began.

On June 28, the forty-first day of the siege of Vicksburg, Colonel Leon D. Marks was mortally wounded by a Union "parrot bomb," which exploded in midair above him. Though he had risked his life in battle on numerous occasions, Colonel Marks was, in the end, struck down as he peacefully ate his dinner.

After the fall of Vicksburg on July 4, the wounded colonel was brought back to Shreveport, where he could be near his wife and son, Frank. While he seemed to be recovering gradually, the injuries to his head were too traumatic and on September 23, 1863, he died. He was thirty-four years old and left a twenty-three-year-old widow and a four-year-old son.

Colonel Leon Dawson Marks was buried on September 24 in his in-laws' plot at Oakland Cemetery. According to his obituary, "The funeral cortege, with military honors and numbers of sympathizing citizens, gave the best evidence of the respect and veneration our people feel for the memory of the soldier who willingly died in defense of his country."

Although his devotion to Judaism appears to have been somewhat tenuous, Marks appears to have maintained connections with the Jewish community of Shreveport, even while attending services of the Presbyterian church with his wife. Marks is regarded as one of only three Jews from Louisiana to attain the rank of colonel in the Confederate army, the others being Colonel Solomon Kursheedt of New Orleans and Colonel Samuel Meyers Hyams of Natchitoches.

Amelia Marks eventually married T. Lytt Lyon of New Orleans, a Confederate veteran. On the night of February 12, 1869, she and her son were traveling with Lyon aboard the ill-fated steamboat *Mittie Stephens*, which caught fire and sank in the murky waters of Caddo Lake en route from Shreveport to Jefferson, Texas. Twenty-nine-year-old Amelia and her son were among the dead; Lyon survived. They were laid to rest next to Colonel Marks at Oakland Cemetery.

General E. Kirby Smith, Confederate Commander

General Edmund Kirby Smith, commander of the Trans-Mississippi Department of the Confederate army, headquartered at Shreveport during the Civil War, was born in St. Augustine, Florida, in 1824. Educated in Virginia and at West Point, where he was nicknamed "Seminole," he was commissioned in the infantry upon his graduation in 1845.

Serving in the Mexican War, Smith won the brevet of first lieutenant for gallantry at Cerro Gordo and was brevetted captain for gallantry at Contreras. During the Mexican War, he lost his older brother, Ephraim Kirby Smith, who was killed at Molino del Rey in 1847. In 1849, Smith became a professor of mathematics at West Point, remaining in that

General E. Kirby Smith.
Author's collection.

post until 1852. Later, he served in the Indian campaigns and on the Texas frontier. In 1861, as a major in the Second Cavalry, he refused to surrender Fort Colorado, Texas, to the Texas militia. Despite this act of loyalty to the Union, Smith eventually resigned his commission, entering Confederate service with the rank of lieutenant colonel upon the secession of Florida.

Early in the Civil War, he served under General J.E. Johnston in the Shenandoah, but in June 1861, he was commissioned brigadier general in the Provisional Army. In July 1861, he was severely wounded at the first Battle of Manassas (also known as the first Battle of Bull Run), and in October he was promoted to major general.

In 1862, Smith was placed in command of the District of East Tennessee, participating in General Bragg's invasion of Kentucky, recovering the Cumberland Gap and winning important victories at Richmond and Perryville, Kentucky. In October 1862, Smith was promoted to lieutenant general and at the end of 1862 was placed in command of the Trans-Mississippi Department, covering much of Louisiana as well as Arkansas, Texas, New Mexico and the Indian Territory (today's Oklahoma). Initially locating his headquarters at Little Rock, he moved them to Shreveport on March 7, 1863. Early in 1864, he received the permanent rank of general in the Provisional Army of the Confederacy, and in the spring of that year he successfully repelled the Red River expedition of Union general Nathaniel P. Banks, despite his forces being outnumbered two to one. Because of his leadership, the city of Shreveport, then the capital of Louisiana, was never captured by Federal forces.

At Shreveport, General Smith wielded far greater power than any other individual, including the governor or any civil officials. Wishing to clean up what he initially called "a miserable place with a miserable population," he organized his own treasury department, post office and cotton bureau, which purchased cotton for four cents per pound and sold it to foreign customers, via Mexico, for fifty cents per pound. It is estimated that a profit of some $125 million in gold came into Shreveport as a result of these cotton maneuvers (some thirty times that in today's dollars). Every cent of this money went to buy arms, medicine and foodstuffs for the Confederacy, including quantities of grain and beef unheard of elsewhere in the, by then, largely impoverished Confederate States.

Never a personal proponent of the "states' rights" ideal that fueled much of the South's fervor for independence, Smith believed that the key to victory lay in greater government centralization within the Confederacy. For this view, as well as others, he frequently butted heads with Confederate general Richard Taylor, also a sometime Shreveporter, who was solidly in the states' rights camp. General Smith's application of the principle of centralization of power to his own seat of command, nationalizing much property for the common good, often found him at odds with the civilian government. As a result, General Smith was much criticized, though under his command Shreveport became one of the most important financial and trading centers of the South during the later part of the war.

On May 26, 1865, forty-seven days after the surrender of the Confederate States at Appomattox Court House in Virginia, the Trans-Mississippi Department of the Confederate army also capitulated. Although the surrender to Union general E.R.S. Canby did not take place in Shreveport, the Trans-Mississippi was nevertheless the last major Rebel command to surrender and Shreveport was the last Confederate seat of government to be returned to the Union.

Interestingly, it was for the Trans-Mississippi Department's headquarters at Shreveport that Confederate president Jefferson Davis was bound when captured in Georgia on May 10, 1865, since at the time it appeared that Shreveport was still a safe haven, with General Smith showing no sign of intending to surrender. In only a little over a fortnight, however, with soldiers deserting en masse and civilians raiding government storehouses and military depots, the inevitable surrender did, in fact, occur. On June 6, 1865, Federal occupation troops entered Shreveport; they would remain until January 29, 1876.

After the war's close, General Smith initially went to Cuba but returned to the United States within a few months. Entering the business world, he became president of the Pacific and Atlantic Telegraph Company, a position he retained for two years. He refused the then-staggering offer of $50,000 per year to serve as president of the Louisiana State Lottery Company, despite having to support a family of eleven children, because he did not wish to be associated with an organization that had a reputation of being notoriously corrupt.

Later, he served as president of the Western Military Academy at Nashville, then as chancellor of the University of Nashville. From 1875 until his death in 1893, he was professor of mathematics at the University of the South in Sewanee, Tennessee, an institution of higher learning founded by another figure from Shreveport history (and a fellow Confederate general), Leonidas Polk.

General Smith died at Sewanee, the last of the Confederacy's eight full generals to succumb, on March 28, 1893, and was buried at the Sewanee City Cemetery on March 31. In 1895, an imposing monument was erected over his grave, the funding for which was raised by contributions from all over the nation, especially from the South and some even from that "miserable place with a miserable population" that he called home through most of the war—Shreveport.

SAMUEL ARMSTEAD, RECONSTRUCTION-ERA SECRETARY OF STATE

Sam Armstead's name is not familiar to most Louisianans today, yet he was once an important figure in the state's—and especially Shreveport's—history. Born into slavery in western Virginia (now part of West Virginia), probably in 1804, he first came to the Shreveport area in 1858 as the property of Dr. William Ball, according to his obituary. He appears to have been in Georgia for a time prior to coming to Louisiana but the duration of his residence there unknown.

Known as Samuel Ball before the Civil War, after emancipation he took the name Joseph Samuel Armstead, though he was best known simply as Sam Armstead. Able to read and write, which was rare for a slave, Sam enjoyed a certain degree of freedom in his middle age, serving as the minister to slaves for the First Methodist Episcopal Church of Shreveport (now First United Methodist Church).

In 1865, he founded the St. Paul African Methodist Episcopal Zion Church (now St. Paul United Methodist Church), leading ninety fellow former slaves who had previously been associated with First Methodist to establish the new congregation. Additionally, at the same time he founded the St. Paul Christian School of the Bottoms, better known at the time as the Christian Bottom School, the first school for black children in Shreveport. The private school, which operated under the auspices of St. Paul Methodist Church, educated black children and taught their parents, most of whom were former slaves, to read and write as well.

The only known photograph of the Reverend Samuel Amstead, made circa 1875. *Author's collection.*

The Reverend Armstead served as pastor of St. Paul's through 1871 and was the church's minister when its second edifice was built in the 600 block of Caddo Street in 1869. The church, which possessed a tall bell tower, became the official timekeeper of the city of Shreveport, its chimes signaling noon each day. It remained the official timekeeper and emergency signal beacon for the city until 1880, when the First Baptist Church completed a new building on Texas Street that had a clock installed in its tower.

St. Paul's Methodist Church remained on Caddo Street until 1926, when the present building was completed on Pierre Avenue and Looney Street (on the site of the old Christian Bottom School). While on Caddo, the church gave its name to the topographically low-lying neighborhood known as "the Bottom," which became known over time as St. Paul's Bottoms, a name it retains to a degree even yet.

In 1870, Sam Armstead was elected to the Louisiana House of Representatives representing Caddo Parish, serving in this capacity through 1871. A year later, he was elected secretary of state of Louisiana on the ticket of Governor Henry Clay Warmoth. Serving into 1873, he was ultimately forced from office, as was the entire Warmoth administration. Nevertheless, for a time he was among the highest ranking black political figures in the state, together with Caesar C. Antoine (also of Shreveport), Pinckney B.S. Pinchback and Oscar J. Dunn.

Returning to Shreveport, Armstead opened a restaurant on the riverfront at the foot of Travis Street. Located near the wharves, the steamboat landing and busy batture area known as "the Strand," the restaurant operated through much of the 1880s. During his days as a restaurateur and after he remained a part-time Methodist minister, performing weddings, funerals, baptisms and other ceremonies and filling in for the regular pastors at the church he had helped establish.

The Reverend Armstead was married twice, first to Catherine Armstead. Born a slave in Louisiana about 1820, she worked with her husband in running the restaurant and was its cook. When they were married is unclear but their children were grown prior to the 1870 census, by which time only the youngest, eighteen-year-old Kate, was still living at home. Throughout this period, teachers from the school also frequently lived with the Armsteads, as did some of their grandchildren. Catherine died at the Armstead home at 612 Caddo Street on March 12, 1891.

The second Mrs. Samuel Armstead was Ann Brown, a local native much younger than her husband. Possibly a teacher, Ann and Sam were married on March 16, 1893. Ann was not quite thirty-three and Sam was about eighty-nine. The couple moved to 101 Louisiana Street shortly after their marriage, later moving down the block to 113, where they resided for the rest of their marriage and where Ann remained for a few years after Sam's death.

Sam Armstead lived another fifteen years after his second wedding. He died at his home on October 4, 1908, at the age of 104. At the time of his death, he was believed to have been the oldest person living in Shreveport or Caddo Parish and perhaps in the state of Louisiana.

Available census records vary as to Sam Armstead's exact age. The Reverend Armstead himself believed that he was born in 1804, and a photograph of him purportedly made about 1871 definitely shows a man appearing to be at least in his sixties then. The official death index for the City of Shreveport shows him to have been 104 at the time of his death, as does his death certificate. His attending physician, Dr. G.A. Cain, also cites 104 as the age he believed Armstead to be.

Samuel Armstead was a minister, an educator, a politician, a restaurant owner and a friend to thousands, both black and white. He rose from slavery to a seat in the state legislature and then to one of the state's highest offices. He was buried at Shreveport's Star Cemetery a few days after his death, yet the grave of this remarkable man is unmarked. Although the exact spot where he rests may never be known, the Star Cemetery Preservation Society has expressed interest in placing a monument to Samuel Armstead at the cemetery. Such would be a fitting tribute to Louisiana's only black secretary of state and a man who lived so long a life in which he did so much for so many.

Aleck Boarman, Youngest Mayor, Oldest Federal Judge

The name Aleck Boarman is not well known these days but a century ago his was one of the most widely recognized and most respected names in the Shreveport area. His story is also one of the city's most interesting biographies.

Judge Alexander John Boarman Jr., better known as "Aleck," was born just outside Yazoo City, Mississippi, on December 10, 1839, the son of

Judge Aleck Boarman, 1881. *Courtesy of the U.S. District Court for the Western District of Louisiana.*

Mr. and Mrs. A. John Boarman of Yazoo County. At the age of six, Boarman came to Shreveport with his parents; here his father and uncle ran a livery stable. In 1849, his father was elected to the city council for a single term.

As his family was not well-to-do, Boarman attended the public schools of Shreveport, though he later was accepted as a cadet at the Kentucky Military Institute. Afterward he attended the University of Kentucky at Lexington, graduating in 1860. Returning to Shreveport, he began to read law in the offices of Benjamin Hodge and F.D. Austin, but his studies were interrupted by the outbreak of war. He joined the Caddo Rifles, Company A, First Regiment, Louisiana Volunteers, as a lieutenant and later was promoted to the company's captain. By war's end, he had attained the rank of major in the Army of Northern Virginia.

After the war, Boarman resumed his law studies, and in 1866 he was admitted to the Louisiana bar. He did not begin his practice immediately, however. On May 7, 1866, at twenty-six years of age, Aleck Boarman was elected mayor of Shreveport, the youngest person ever to hold that office. During Mayor Boarman's tenure, the city purchased its first steam fire engine, which was named Caddo Number One, and signaled the birth of the modern city fire department. Although popular, Boarman served as mayor for one term only, not seeking reelection. In 1868, he was elected for a single term to the city council during the administration of his successor as mayor, Lewis S. Markham. Later that year, Markham's successor, Martin Tally, appointed Boarman city attorney, a position he retained for the next four years.

On December 3, 1872, Boarman was elected on the Democratic ticket to the U.S. House of Representatives, representing the Fourth Congressional District of Louisiana until March 3, 1873. His election filled the seat left vacant by the death of James McCleery in the Forty-second Congress.

Returning to private legal practice in 1873, Boarman set up offices on Market Street at Milam. Surviving the yellow fever epidemic of 1873, which carried off nearly one thousand citizens, he continued in practice another four years until being elected judge of the state's tenth judicial district court at Caddo Parish, a post in which he remained through 1880.

On May 18, 1881, President James A. Garfield appointed Boarman (by then a Republican—rare around here in those days, especially for an ex-

Confederate officer) judge of the newly created U.S. District Court for the Western District of Louisiana, which was created by act of Congress on March 3, 1881. Initially, the Western District comprised nearly the whole of Louisiana west of the Mississippi River; the seat of the court was set at Shreveport (in 1888 it was split into five divisions). The federal court was housed in rooms on the upper floor of the Utz and Smith Building, 513 Spring Street, today known as the Harrison Building.

Not until 1887 was the first federal courthouse ready for occupancy. Located at 424 Texas Street, it housed all federal government offices (including the main post office) and had a single courtroom on the third floor. That building survived only until 1911, when a larger federal building, now the main branch of the Shreve Memorial Library system, was built on the same site. Judge Boarman oversaw the construction of both federal buildings.

A bachelor most of his life, Aleck Boarman was finally married on November 29, 1898, to Frances Capon. He was a few days shy of his fifty-ninth birthday at the time. The marriage was brief, however, for Frances died fewer than four years later, in 1902, and was buried with her family in the Bellefontaine Cemetery in St. Louis, Missouri (where Captain Henry Miller Shreve, the principal founder of Shreveport, is also buried). Boarman survived her by fourteen years and never married again. On August 30, 1916, while vacationing at Loon Lake, New York, Judge Boarman was stricken with heart failure and died at the age of seventy-six. At the time, he was the oldest sitting federal judge in the nation.

Judge Boarman was buried in the Elstner family plot at Oakland Cemetery, next to U.S. attorney Milton C. Elstner and his wife (Judge Boarman's cousin), Julia Smoker Elstner, daughter of Judge Boarman's aunt, Martha Boarman Smoker. A large granite marker on his grave reads only "Aleck Boarman, United States Judge, 1839–1916."

BUILDERS AND DEVELOPERS

Norman Davis, Early Civic Developer

At the very northern edge of Shreveport's Highland area is a small road called Davis Street. Barely qualifying as passable, it runs between Marshall Street and a point just east of Louisiana Avenue in the old Holmesville area that borders Highland on the south and downtown on the north. At one time, it ran farther west than its present length, extending all the way to the intersection of Line Avenue and Howell Street (now part of Fairfield), but the construction of Interstate 20 in the early 1960s eliminated its westernmost blocks. It is unfortunate that Davis Street is so inconspicuous and in such a poor state of repair, for behind its name lies a fascinating and important story.

Davis Street is named for one of Shreveport's earliest developers and one of the very first to subdivide property outside the original grid laid out by the Shreve Town Company in 1836. What is even more significant, especially considering the era in which he lived, is that he was black.

Norman Davis was born in Virginia in 1800. Very little is known of his early life except that he was of mixed parentage. Sometime around the age of forty-five he settled in Shreveport, where he practiced the trade of a barber, operating N. Davis's Shaving and Hair Dressing Shop on the south side of the 200 block of Texas Street, about where part of the old CNB/United Mercantile Building stands today. Next door was the Powell Hotel and nearby were other hotels, ensuring a steady trade. By the late 1840s, Davis's shop was a regular advertiser in the *Caddo Gazette* newspaper, though he himself never learned to read and write, signing all legal documents with an "X."

The 1850 census shows the Davis family as representing five of the twenty-one "free persons of color," as free blacks were called, living in Shreveport at the time. Davis's wife, Catherine, was born a slave in Mississippi in 1810, her freedom presumably purchased by her husband. They had three children, all natives of Louisiana: Christopher (b. 1833), Sally Ann (b. 1838) and William Nelson (b. 1842). William Nelson Davis would later, like his father, become a barber and real estate developer.

In 1848, David purchased a ten-acre tract of land just west of what is now the central business district of Shreveport. Beginning in 1849, he subdivided it into thirty-one lots, fifteen of which were sold by 1851, all to well-to-do white Shreveporters. The area of this initial development was what is now Austin Place, Grand Avenue and the 900 block of Texas Avenue. In 1866, when Texas Avenue was widened to its present width, Davis sold the right of way on either side of the 900 block to the city for $800 (around $20,000 in today's terms).

In addition to his real estate developing, Davis was also the leader of one of Shreveport's first musical ensembles, the Royal Ethiopian Band. The band was made up of both freemen of color and slaves and played at many early social functions. The *Caddo Gazette* in 1853 described the city's earliest known debutante ball and mentioned "Old Norman" playing his "soul-stirring violin."

The Royal Ethiopian Band in 1849 was exempted by the city council from the 9:00 p.m. curfew imposed upon slaves. Members of the band at the time were Isaac Johnson, Jim Brown, Billy Field, Robin Moore and Norman Davis, all freemen, and Henry, Mike, Joe and another Norman, all slaves. Little to nothing is known about these men, apart from Davis.

It is interesting to observe the levels of cooperation and camaraderie between the races and between bondmen and freemen during the pre–Civil War years. Free blacks were treated by their white neighbors essentially as equals, while slaves obviously were not. Yet free blacks treated enslaved blacks as equals. Slaves who had special skills, such as those of the Royal Ethiopian Band members, could thus earn an income, and some could use this money toward purchasing their freedom.

In any case, Davis also engaged in partnerships with white property owners, hiring the city surveyor, G.D. Jones, to divide their property into lots, upon which Davis would then build houses for speculation. Parts of the Crosstown and Bluegoose areas were thus developed, in part through partnerships between Norman Davis and landowners such as Walker Carter (Henry Shreve's son-in-law), Featherstone R. Roach and others. Davis Street was one of two streets named in Davis's honor. The other was Norman Street, which connected Texas Avenue to Snow Street. Today it is known as Wilson Street, a name it received informally in the late nineteenth century because a single family named Wilson owned all the land fronting the street. After the murder of Shreveport police patrolman Charles Wilson, a son of the same family, in 1896, the name became formalized. Exactly a century later, the street was closed at the railroad crossing, and since that time it has been known simply as Wilson Alley.

In any event, Norman Davis spent the years 1866, 1867 and part of 1868 dividing his time between Shreveport and Galveston, Texas. Why he spent so much time in Galveston is uncertain, but it is known that he also owned land in the vicinity. Catherine Davis and the children remained in Shreveport during Norman's time in Texas. In May 1868, Norman Davis died in Galveston.

Rarely during the tumultuous and racially charged period of Reconstruction did white-owned southern newspapers give lengthy or laudatory obituaries to blacks, but the former pro-Confederate Shreveport paper *Southwestern* did just that for Norman Davis on May 20, 1868. Additionally, according to the *Southwestern*, Davis left an estate valued at some $120,000 (approximately $3 million in today's terms), an enormous amount for anyone of either race at the time. This included his barbershop, his real estate and other property holdings in and around Shreveport and rural land in Texas as well.

William N. Davis continued on his father's path. It was he who named the two streets in Norman Davis's honor. Later, he and his mother also sold the right of way parallel to Texas Avenue where it crossed Norman Street to the Southern Pacific Railroad. It is now used by Kansas City Southern.

The story of Norman Davis is one that deserves to be remembered. Like a later black developer, Colonel Giles Moore, who in the 1920s built Shreveport's Mooretown area, Davis left a legacy still present in Shreveport, a remarkable and rare success for a black man in those days and a testament to his talent, his ability to overcome the odds stacked against him and his business acumen.

A.C. STEERE: BUILDER OF NEIGHBORHOODS

To most Shreveporters, the name A.C. Steere is best known as that borne by the conspicuous yet charming old Mediterranean Revival–style elementary school on Youree Drive at Ockley. But the man A.C. Steere, who gave the land for that school (originally called the Broadmoor School) in 1929, helped shape the development of Shreveport in a way few others have.

Albert Colwell Steere was born in 1879, the son of Cyrus and Johnette Steere. As a child, his family resided in a large Victorian home at the southwest corner of Fairfield and Margaret Place; later they moved a few blocks away to Southern Avenue. Like his father, A.C. Steere entered the real estate business, though in addition he was to become a real estate developer.

"Steere-built homes are well built homes" was Steere's motto, and during the height of his real estate development career, the 1910s and 1920s, Steere built whole neighborhoods, laying out their streets and accomplishing their annexation into the city. Some of these projects he financed himself and others were built with partners. Perhaps his most noteworthy partnership was that with Elias Goldstein, with whom he developed the South Highlands Fairfield Heights and Glen Iris neighborhoods.

Steere also developed the Broadmoor neighborhood on the site of the old Peter Youree plantation. Indeed, he named its principal thoroughfare, Youree Drive, in Captain Youree's honor. Dixie Garden was another Steere development, this time with a more rural approach. To this day, Dixie Garden retains the rural feel Steere envisioned for the area a century ago. From lower-income neighborhoods, such as Stoner Hill and Hollywood, to upper-income areas, such as Glen Iris and the Thornhill section of Highland, Steere built homes for the whole spectrum of Shreveport's citizens.

Additionally, Steere was a philanthropist. Not only did he donate the Broadmoor School site, as mentioned previously, but Betty Virginia Park was also given to the city by him and his partner Goldstein in honor of their daughters, Betty Goldstein (later Franklin) and Virginia Steere (later Marston). Virginia Steere was named after her mother, Virginia Collins Steere. A.C. and Virginia Steere resided in several homes built by Steere throughout his career. For years they lived at 910 Robinson Place, though

A.C. Steere. *Courtesy of LSUS Noel Memorial Library Archives.*

this house, a large and airy frame Arts and Crafts–style home, is now demolished. Later they resided at 939 Delaware and then lastly at 910 Ockley, both of which still stand. Steere also built the Greek Revival–style mansion at 1090 East Kings Highway overlooking Old River Bayou for himself but never lived there, selling it instead to the J.H. Adger family before its completion.

Ockley Drive, developed by Steere, was named for Steere's father's ancestral home in Ockley, Surrey County, England. Other streets in South Highlands and Broadmoor were also named by Steere and reflect his family (for example, Steere, Johnette, Albert, Colwell and Trabue), his friends and associates (Patton, Grover, Zeke and Finley), places his family came from (Ockley and Stratford, England; Albany and Oneonta, New York), places where they vacationed (Broadmoor, Colorado; Monrovia, California; Lakes Ontario and Erie) and historical figures (such as John Charles Fremont and Peter Youree). Thora Boulevard, in South Highlands, was originally named Esplanade Boulevard but was changed by Steere to honor Thora Spence, wife of a business associate.

Steere also was a director of KTBS radio in its early days and was involved in the planning of Barksdale Army Air Field (now Barksdale Air Force Base). He also was largely responsible for inducing the Texas and Pacific Railroad to transfer a major division point from east Texas to Shreveport, and was developer of the Hollywood area of Shreveport as a neighborhood for railroad workers and their families. He chaired the city's real estate board for several years and was a central figure on the building committee of the First Presbyterian Church when it moved from Travis Street (where the Beck Building now stands) to its present location on Jordan Street in 1926. He was also a member of the board of directors of the Commercial National Bank.

Steere's untimely and tragic death came as the result of the financial panic that swept the nation following the crash of the stock market in October 1929. In the summer of 1930, Steere believed himself to be financially ruined and on Tuesday, July 1 of that year, he committed suicide. Early that morning, he shot himself through the heart as he sat next to the swimming pool at his Ockley Drive home (his was one of the city's very first private swimming pools; it was located at the rear of the property before that part of the estate was subdivided to build Betty

Virginia Park). Steere had panicked, however, and acted rashly. He was not ruined after all, as it turned out, but merely set back considerably. His company would not have to declare bankruptcy, as he had feared. Unfortunately, by the time others learned the truth it was too late for A.C. Steere.

Steere's death came as a tremendous shock to the city. KTBS radio went silent at noon the day of his death out of respect and mourning. On July 2, Steere was buried in the Masonic section of Greenwood Cemetery, next to his son, A.C. Steere Jr., who had died in 1915 at the age of three. Steere's widow would survive another twelve years, his daughter another thirty-nine. Eventually, the Broadmoor School was renamed in his honor. Today it is listed in the National Register of Historic Places, partly for its superb architectural design and partly for its connections with one of Shreveport's and Louisiana's most influential civic developers of the early twentieth century.

Bettie LaCals, the Black Woman Who Helped Create South Highlands

The name of Bettie Parsons LaCals is not a household phrase by any means. Nevertheless, Mrs. LaCals played an important role in the development of the South Highlands area, one of Shreveport's premier neighborhoods. Especially interesting, however, is the fact that Mrs. LaCals was a black woman. What follows is her story:

Bettie Parsons LaCals was born prior to the Civil War, though precisely when is uncertain; evidently it was about the mid-1850s. Whether she was born a slave is also uncertain, especially since her ancestry was mixed. When she was in her midteens, she married Mark Parsons, also of mixed white and African American parentage, whose mother, Frances, though it appears she was born a slave, had been a "free woman of color" for some time prior to the Civil War. Through unknown sources, probably an inheritance from her master (who was also likely Mark's father), Frances Parsons had amassed a sizeable savings.

In 1866, Mrs. Parsons bought ten acres of land from Captain Leroy Moncure Nutt, owner of Fairfield Hill plantation (located where Mall St. Vincent stands today). This tract consisted of most of a city block at Travis and Common Streets, including "all the buildings and improvements thereon." Nutt, who had owned the property for thirteen years, was paid $1,000 (about $30,000 to $40,000 in today's money) in gold coin for the property by Mrs. Parsons, who signed the documents with an X.

About 1879, Frances Parsons died. The following year Mark, who inherited the Travis at Common site, turned it all over to his wife, Bettie. Three years later, Bettie used some of the rental profit from this land to purchase seventy-nine acres south of town for $1,000. Later, this land was to become the nucleus of the South Highlands neighborhood. At the time she purchased it, however, the land was largely wooded and unbuilt except for a log house and a small cemetery. The cemetery contained only two marked graves, those of John (d. 1871) and Cynthia Ball Walpole (d. 1870). It is thought, however, that there were more burials there than only these two.

In any case, Bettie continued to purchase land, including more downtown and Allendale area property, all of which was quite profitable. There was a fly in the ointment, however. Bettie seems to have had a bad habit of ignoring property tax bills. In 1889, her Shreveport home was sold to L.E. Carter at a tax sale, though Carter allowed her to stay on in the house as a renter at a rate of eight dollars per month, which even then was cheap; she was always lucky that way.

Mark Parsons, meanwhile, was in business in his own right. He operated a café on Texas Avenue and sold produce raised on Bettie's property at the city market, a public, twenty-four-hour market much like the old French market of New Orleans. In 1889, Mark died, leaving his land and business to Bettie.

Later, Bettie married Henry LaCals, a mixed-race blacksmith, who came to live with her in her home on what is now Delaware Street. In 1908, Line Avenue was extended across the eastern edge of her property. For the right of way, the parish paid her one dollar plus ten more for every sixteen and a half feet of linear roadway. This doesn't sound like much, but it was actually far better than the going rate for rights of way—many landowners got nothing.

In 1912, Albert C. Steere and his development companies bought nineteen acres from Bettie for $6,000 (about $175,000 in today's money). Considering her purchase of the full seventy-nine acres in 1883 for $1,000, this was a substantial profit. In 1913, Steere bought fifty more acres from her for $33,000 (about $850,000 in today's money).

Thus, Bettie Parsons LaCals still had ten of her original seventy-nine acres and a solid profit of $38,000—the greater part of $1 million today. She moved her little house from Delaware Street to what is now Walton Place, a few blocks away. In 1917, she sold the water rights to the land on Walton for $100 per year to Steere, who built the Cedar Grove/South Highlands waterworks just behind her home; several attractive town houses occupy the site today.

In 1925, the LaCals sold a small lot from her remaining ten acres for $350, and in 1928 sold the remaining eight and sixty-four one-hundredths acres of the original seventy-nine to Steere for $7,500. Steere generously allowed the LaCals to remain on the property rent-free for life and even to farm a small section of surrounding property for their own use. Despite having made a fortune through her real estate investments, especially by the standards of the day, Bettie Parsons LaCals died in poverty on April 8, 1935.

What happened to the enormous profit she reaped from her sale of land to A.C. Steere? How did this woman, who in her youth had been able to amass a sizeable estate and become a significant landowner in the parish, manage to spend so substantial a profit in a twenty-three-year period yet have nothing to show for it? That we shall never know.

In any case, there was not even enough money for a funeral, and indeed, she even left debts! Carrie Williams, wife of undertaker J.S. Williams, paid for the burial out of her own pocket. Mrs. LaCals was buried at the old Hopewell Cemetery at the east end of the 500 block of East Merrick Street in Stoner Hill, an area also developed by Steere. In 1957, the graves in the Walpole Cemetery were moved to Forest Park and a house was built on the site (the southeast corner of Monrovia and Thornhill). The LaCals house, formerly the Walpole home, was torn down about 1936.

Colonel Giles Moore and the Suburb He Built

The area of Shreveport known as Mooretown has a long and interesting history. The neighborhood actually developed in several stages beginning in the second decade of the twentieth century, the earliest portion being the area around Broadway and Cleveland/Henry Street, just west of Jewella Avenue and east of what is now Kennedy Drive.

The original developer of Mooretown was a man named Giles D. Moore, known as "Colonel Moore," a Shreveport schoolteacher who began

Colonel Giles D. Moore.
Courtesy of Professor Willie Burton, Shreveport, Louisiana.

acquiring real estate in 1898. By the 1910s, Moore was the principal black realtor and developer in Shreveport, with offices located in a building at Texas Avenue and Lawrence Street in Allendale. The building, which still stands, was in one of the blocks of Texas Avenue that constituted the black business district of Shreveport in those days and was known simply as "The Avenue." Here he also had an apartment where he resided between about 1902 and 1906, when he purchased a house at 942 Pickett Street in the Crosstown neighborhood. Years before, in the 1890s, he had lived at 1040 Pickett, a bit farther up, while still a young schoolteacher. In 1910, he moved to a farm he acquired off what is now Broadway Street. A few years later, he began to subdivide his land into a new community.

Up until that time, Colonel Moore had been primarily concerned with property sales in the Allendale and St. Paul's Bottoms areas of Shreveport. Moore's Town, as Mooretown was originally known, would be quite different. Moore was an admirer of the black unification leader Marcus Garvey and admired Garvey's social theories. Garvey founded the

Universal Negro Improvement Association in 1914, which urged black people to stand up for their civil rights, establish a true pride in both their race and themselves and become economically independent. Garvey's philosophies were laid out in his weekly newspaper, the *Negro World*, to which Colonel Moore subscribed. Moore agreed with Garvey's assertion that black equality would come to pass only when black people became economically independent.

To this end, Colonel Moore decided to establish a "colored town," as he called it: a community built and run entirely by and for black people. He envisioned it ultimately becoming an incorporated community with its own city government, businesses, churches, factories and schools—in short, a black suburb of Shreveport where its residents would be first-class citizens, equal in every way to their white counterparts in the city. Pride of ownership in their own homes and property, Moore felt, would liberate his people and bring them respect both from others and from themselves.

Although Mooretown never became an autonomous incorporated town, for many years it did function very much like one, with Colonel Moore its de facto mayor. Its school, now the Bethune School, was established early on, and about 1920, a ten-thousand-plot cemetery called Zion Rest was laid out and dedicated on Henry Street at what was then the edge of the community. Many of Mooretown's original residents and developers, including Colonel Moore, are buried at Zion Rest, which is still a functioning cemetery today.

Nearby to Mooretown were the huge U.S. Sheet and Window Glass Company's plant and the National Gasoline and Refrigeration Company refinery, two of the area's largest employers, both locating there during the 1920s. These would later become Libbey Glass and the Atlas Processing Company, respectively. Numerous Mooretown residents were employed by these firms, which were within a short walking distance of their homes. Likewise, the railroad was close, as was the highway to Shreveport and Greenwood. The Jewella Road ran to the nearby community of Jewella and to Cross Lake.

Nearby, in the 1920s, A.C. Steere laid out the Hollywood neighborhood. Steere, though white, embraced Colonel Moore's philosophy of black equality and pride of ownership and likewise patterned his development to ensure that all properties were owner-occupied and not sold as rentals. Moore's influence (and, ironically, that of Garvey, who was viewed with suspicion by the white establishment in America at that time) was far reaching.

Mooretown had its own groceries, churches, cafés and other businesses, many of them concentrated on Hollywood, Jewella and Cleveland Streets but also scattered throughout. It never developed a utility infrastructure, however. Residents used wells and septic tanks, and open sewers were a problem for many years. Not all homes had electrical service and telephone service was spotty. Not until the 1950s, when Mooretown was annexed to Shreveport, were universal water and sewerage service, electrical and gas service and public transportation brought to Mooretown. Nevertheless, the community managed on its own for three decades as an unincorporated community. Even without reliable utilities or city services, the fact that Mooretown not only survived but indeed thrived is a remarkable testimony to Colonel Moore and the people who participated in his social experiment. In Moore's Town, there were no renters, only property owners. Moore even set up the land bank that carried the paper on the properties he sold. Even the mortgages in Mooretown were self-contained; nothing was dependent upon outside parties.

On December 4, 1929, Colonel Moore, who had never married, died. His nephew settled his estate, which, in today's dollars, made Moore a multimillionaire. At the time of his death, Giles Moore owned nearly a quarter of all of Mooretown, which brought him a regular income as rental property. But this was not regular rental property; all was rent to own. Ultimately, every renter of Moore's was to become a homeowner, and under the covenants of the community, no one was able to purchase property specifically for the purpose of rental income. In addition to land in the Mooretown development, Colonel Moore also owned undeveloped land to the north of the neighborhood, in the vicinity of the Shreveport Country Club, as well as in north Shreveport and to the west of Mooretown. Not at all bad for a black ex-schoolteacher born into abject poverty of ex-slave parents during Reconstruction.

After Colonel Moore's untimely death, the Mooretown neighborhood was expanded several times. In the mid-1950s, during the administration of Mayor James Gardner and as Shreveport was moving continually westward, Mooretown was formally annexed to the city, receiving city utilities and public transportation for the first time. A boom in new houses along Broadway and west of Kennedy Drive began, continuing through the next thirty years. The Mooretown Annex, south of Hollywood

Avenue, which had begun in the 1920s, was substantially expanded and improved during the 1950s and 1960s. Many of its streets are named for important figures from black history such as Booker T. Washington, George Washington Carver, Medgar Evers, Joe Louis and the Reverend Roy Mayfield, who brought Coleman College's campus to Mooretown in 1946.

Coleman College, founded at Gibsland, Louisiana, in 1887, was the first black institution of higher learning in northwestern Louisiana. In 1942, it came to Shreveport, and four years later its campus was built on Hollywood Avenue and Jewella, where Winnfield Funeral Home is today. Coleman College lasted only a decade in Mooretown, but its presence helped make the area around Hollywood and Jewella Avenues the neighborhood's "downtown," which to some degree it remains to this day.

The people of Mooretown continue to take pride in their area, just as they did when Colonel Moore first laid out his town a century ago. The neighborhood has grown markedly since that time, and even today the majority of the homes in Mooretown are owner-occupied. Colonel Giles D. Moore would doubtless be very proud of the success of his town, even though it is now part of the larger city and no longer an autonomous community.

Justin Gras, Civic Leader and Philanthropist

In the 500 block of Louisiana Street is a large and imposing red brick building trimmed with limestone and cast iron. Best known as the longtime location of Gilmore's News Stand, which operated there through very nearly the whole of the twentieth century, this structure is otherwise called the Gras Building. In fact, if one looks carefully, the words "Justin Gras 1900" can be seen carved at the very top of the building's façade.

The builder of this structure, Justin Vincent Gras, was at one time the largest individual property owner in Shreveport. Additionally, he owned commercial property in New Orleans and farmland in southwest Caddo Parish and was a major stockholder in Paramount Pictures, General Motors and dozens of railroads and utilities. He was also part owner of the Slattery Building, the city's largest office building at the time of its construction in the early 1920s, and was once the owner of the property upon which Byrd High School now stands.

Justin Gras (center) with his nieces Evette Thompson (left) and Antoinette Emmer in front of his store, June 1956. *Photo by J. Frank McAneny. Author's collection.*

It was not always so, however. A native of the Alpine town of Embrun, France, Gras left home in 1891, at the age of twenty-three, to assist his uncle, Justin Ricou, a Shreveport grocer who had lost his son, twenty-year-old Justin Jr., a year before. Ricou had come to America years before with the intention of going on to Rio de Janeiro, Brazil. He never made it past Louisiana, however. Here he entered into the grocery and liquor business, married the widow of a local merchant, also of French descent (Catherine Larmier Danbreun), and settled down to raise a family.

When Justin Gras arrived in Shreveport, he spoke no English. Within four years, however, he was adept enough both at the English language and the grocery business to set out on his own. Opening a small store at the southwest corner of Texas Avenue and Common Street in 1895, Gras began what was to become the largest retail grocery and liquor business in Shreveport. By 1900, he had begun to invest in commercial real estate, building the 525 Louisiana Street building that still bears his name. Shortly thereafter, he brought two brothers, a sister, a brother-in-law and a niece over from France.

Noted for his philanthropy, Gras contributed liberally to charitable causes beginning even before he was wealthy. His oft-repeated motto was "what's good for Shreveport is good for me," and he became famous for living up to that maxim. Gras was a benefactor of Centenary College, St. Vincent's and St. Mary's schools, the French Benevolent Society and other groups and institutions. He helped found the Shreveport Chamber of Commerce and contributed to the construction of the now historic St. John Berchmans Cathedral.

Nor was his philanthropy limited to Shreveport. For his contributions to French charitable causes, he was awarded the prestigious Palmes Academiques award from the French Ministry of Education, and in 1954 he was given the Benemerenti Award by Pope Pius XII for his contributions to the restoration of the Cathedral of Embrun, built by Charlemagne in the ninth century, and for furnishing funds to rebuild a school and chapel at the village of Le Petit Puy, near Embrun. Part of his estate was later willed to the maintenance of the Le Petit Puy chapel as well as the St. Roch Chapel at Embrun. Other funds went to Centenary, St. John's School, St. John Berchmans Church and St. Vincent Academy in Shreveport.

Perhaps Gras' greatest philanthropic contribution, however, was the establishment of the Community Foundation of Shreveport-Bossier, founded in 1961 according to terms set forth in Gras' will. Gras himself died in 1959 at the age of ninety-one, succumbing to a heart attack at his 630 Elmwood Street home (which is still surrounded by oak trees grown from acorns Gras gathered from the oaks on the courthouse lawn). He was survived by his wife, Eugenie Torr Gras, formerly of San Jose, California. The two met on a cruise in 1925 and married shortly thereafter. Until the age of fifty-seven, Gras had been unmarried. Though his wife was almost twenty years younger than he, the two had no children. At Eugenie's death in 1971, her estate, including the residual portion of Justin Gras' estate that she had inherited, also went to the Community Foundation. Among beneficiaries of the Gras Trust of the Community Foundation have been the Shreveport Symphony, the Strand, LSU in Shreveport, the Red River Revel and many other worthwhile causes.

An interesting story about Gras tells something of his personality. The Gras grocery business flourished for many years, and Gras worked just as hard in his stores as a wealthy old man as he had when he was a struggling young man. Many relatives were also employed by Gras, and his other employees he treated as if they were his relatives. By the mid-1950s, however, Gras was in his eighties, and large supermarket chains were beginning to supplant locally owned businesses like that of Gras. Because his stores were losing money, Gras decided to close his grocery firm in 1955. He kept one store open another year, however, so that one lifelong employee could continue to work there past his sixty-fifth birthday and thus receive full Social Security benefits.

As Justin Gras was in life, so has he been in death, for his philanthropic nature lives on, though he has been dead now for over half a century. He and Eugenie, along with other family members, rest in a large mausoleum at St. Joseph's Catholic Cemetery on Texas Avenue. His spirit, however, can be found in many Shreveport institutions even yet.

J.B. Slattery, City Developer

At the northeast corner of Fairfield Avenue and Dalzell Street stands one of the finest homes on a street lined with many of the city's finest homes. Known by its builder's name, 2401 Fairfield is still called the Slattery House, though it has passed through the hands of three owners since being sold by Slattery family descendants in the early 1990s.

The house was built by John Bernard Slattery, a longtime civic leader and businessman, who also built the Slattery Building in Shreveport's central business district. Born in New York City of Irish parents in 1844, Slattery was raised on a farm near Madison, Wisconsin, where his family moved during his childhood. He was educated there, went to Milton College and in 1872 graduated from the University of Wisconsin law school. Although he was of age to have served in the Civil War, John B. Slattery did not see service, although his father did serve in the Union army.

Upon graduation, Slattery accepted a position, not as a lawyer, but as a teacher in a private academy in Port Gibson, Mississippi. His friends from college days—William McKenna, then postmaster of Shreveport, and Michael Walsh, mayor of Shreveport—urged him to leave Port Gibson and come to Shreveport. When McKenna died suddenly in 1874,

J.B. Slattery. *Courtesy of LSUS Noel Memorial Library Archives.*

Slattery did just that, filling out his friend's unexpired term as postmaster before embarking upon the practice of law here. Both McKenna and Walsh had come to Shreveport with the Union occupation army and had stayed.

From the time of his departure for Port Gibson in 1872 until 1876, John Bernard Slattery carried on a long-distance courtship with Mary Frances Herron, a girl ten years his junior whom he had met while he was a law student and she a coed at the University of Wisconsin. In 1876, the two were married in Wisconsin and came to Shreveport early in 1877 as Mr. and Mrs. Slattery. In his absence, John B. Slattery had been elected district attorney of Caddo Parish, a job that was waiting for him when the newlywed couple arrived here.

Later, Slattery served as assistant clerk of court of Caddo Parish and was prominent in the real estate business. Having great faith in

Shreveport's future, he invested heavily in real estate himself, and by the early twentieth century he was among the largest landowners in Caddo Parish. He also engaged in various business ventures here and was a pioneer in the local oil-refining industry, founding the D'Artois Refining Company with partner George D'Artois (grandfather of Shreveport's widely remembered commissioner of public safety of the same name), who had gained his experience in the oil industry during his youth in Pennsylvania. Sometime later, one of Mr. Slattery's daughters married Mr. D'Artois' son.

In the 1880s, John Bernard Slattery was among the leaders in the successful effort to bring the Texas and Pacific Railroad to Shreveport, and he was later a strong proponent of municipal subsidies to bring the Red River Valley and Kansas City Southern (KCS) Railroads to Shreveport. The huge and vital presence of the KCS Railroad here is due in no small measure to his vision.

Additionally, Slattery was a charter founder and leader of the Shreveport Progressive League and the Shreveport Chamber of Commerce and served on numerous boards and committees of civic, business and church groups, such as the Catholic Knights of America and the Knights of Columbus. He was a longtime member and supporter of Holy Trinity Catholic Church and contributed substantially to the construction of the now historic downtown church in 1896. He later was a founding member of St. John Berchmans Catholic Church in 1902 and was instrumental in acquiring the land for that congregation's first building. He died in 1927, just as plans were being formulated for a new edifice for the church on Jordan Street. Today, the new congregation of Slattery's time is St. John Berchmans Cathedral, seat of the bishop of the diocese of Shreveport. The present cathedral building, then a parish church, was completed in 1929.

For several years, the Slattery family resided on Commerce Street near Texas Street, but about 1890 they purchased a large tract on Fairfield, just at the city limits. This property contained a barracks-like structure and a barn, probably remnants of the Union occupation, during which time troops were billeted along Fairfield south of town. For several years, the family lived in the old barracks with the intention of building a house where the barn stood. A large house was needed, as the Slatterys had twelve children. Their eldest child, John Frances Slattery, who was his father's law partner, decided to build his home right next door to his parents' house. Many people in town openly wondered why the Slatterys would want to live so far out of town, so far from the center of things. Indeed, the location was then rather remote. The farthest streetcar stop in town was a block north of the Slattery property, and the streetcars turned around on the lot next door to John F. Slattery's place. But John B. Slattery, always a visionary, felt sure that the city would continue to grow, and he was right. Within just two more decades, the mansion he erected on his lot near the edge of town would be well within the city limits.

Unfortunately, Mrs. Slattery died in 1901 while her much anticipated home was still in its planning stages. Nevertheless, her husband decided to go ahead and build their dream house, and in 1902 construction commenced. Prominent Shreveport architect Nathaniel Sykes Allen designed the house, and the Garson Brothers contracting firm built it. Late in 1903, the Slattery family moved into the finished house.

Some sources have put the date of the house at 1904 but an early photo of the newly finished home, dated 1903 and labeled "our house" by one of the Slattery children, confirms the earlier date. Also, although the house has all the hallmarks of an N.S. Allen design, the only extant documentary evidence regarding its construction cited the Garson Brothers, a firm that ranked foremost among northwest Louisiana building contractors from the late nineteenth century into the 1930s. The Garson Brothers *built* houses; however, they did not design them. Several years ago, this writer stumbled upon architectural elevations of the Slattery House in the N.S. Allen papers at the LSU-Shreveport Archives, finally proving that Allen designed the place. Presumably, he also designed John Francis Slattery's residence next door, built at the same time as his father's home and also by the Garson Brothers.

Both Slattery houses rank among the city's foremost Victorians, the John B. Slattery House being the largest remaining Victorian home in the city and one of only five standing structures positively attributed to N.S. Allen.

In 1923, John Bernard Slattery built the Gothic Revival downtown building that bears his name. A seventeen-story skyscraper, it was then the tallest and largest capacity building in Shreveport as well as the tallest privately owned building between New Orleans and St. Louis. Until 1940, the Slattery Building remained Shreveport's tallest, and though today dwarfed by much larger buildings, it remains one of downtown Shreveport's most architecturally appealing office buildings and is a cornerstone of the Downtown Historic District. Like the Slattery House, the Slattery Building remained in the hands of heirs of its builder until the last decade of the twentieth century.

Just prior to his death, John Bernard Slattery was planning to develop a large suburban subdivision on land he owned located between what are now Linden Street, Dudley Drive, Line Avenue and Parkway Boulevard. Today, the area is occupied by parts of the Glenwood and Madison Park neighborhoods but then it was open land known as "Slattery's Pasture."

Ideas for a neighborhood on the site had begun to gel in John B. Slattery's mind as early as 1922, but the downtown building filled much of his time and it was not until it was open and largely occupied in 1926 that he began to make serious plans to begin work. Unfortunately, ground was never broken, at least not by Mr. Slattery, who died in September 1927, having already set his plans to paper.

A neighborhood did begin to arise within a year of Slattery's death, but it was built largely by A.C. Steere and the South Highlands–Broadmoor Land Company, which acquired the site from the Slattery heirs. In honor of the man who had owned the land and first planned its development, Slattery Boulevard, which runs through the middle of the neighborhood and is its widest street, was named. The neighborhood itself is formally known as the Slattery Park Subdivision, although it is most widely regarded as being part of the larger South Highlands/Glenwood neighborhood.

Few have left so large a mark on their city as John Bernard Slattery did on Shreveport. His mortal remains rest at St. Joseph Catholic Cemetery on Texas Avenue but his name and legacy live on in the many descendants he and his wife have living here today, in the landmark building that bears his name, in the street and subdivision that also bear his name and in the fabulous wedding cake mansion on Fairfield, which will always be known as the Slattery House.

M.E. Dodd, Minister, Educator and Pioneer Radio Evangelist

One of Shreveport's most prominent and influential figures of the first half of the twentieth century was the Reverend Dr. Monroe Elmon Dodd,

M.E. Dodd, 1920. *Courtesy of First Baptist Church, Shreveport, Louisiana.*

pastor of the First Baptist Church of Shreveport from 1912 to 1950 and pastor emeritus until his death in 1952.

Dodd was born September 8, 1878, near Brazil, Tennessee, and grew up nearby. In 1898, he volunteered for service in the Spanish-American

War, and a year later he entered Union University at Jackson, Tennessee, from which he graduated in 1904. In 1909, his alma mater awarded him an honorary doctorate in divinity and in 1930 an honorary doctorate in letters. He also held two other honorary doctorates, one from Clinton College (1908) and one from Baylor (1918). In 1904, Dodd married Emma Savage, daughter of Dr. George M. Savage, then president of Union University. The couple would eventually become the parents of four daughters and a son.

Before coming to Shreveport in April 1912, Dodd occupied the pulpits of churches in Bolivar, Pinson and Fulton, Tennessee, and in Paducah and Louisville, Kentucky. After coming to Shreveport, Dodd was not only First Baptist's pastor but also served as a chaplain at Camp Beauregard during World War I as well as an army chaplain overseas during that conflict.

Dodd's influence in the Southern Baptist Church was far-reaching. One of the nation's earliest radio evangelists, his broadcasts over Shreveport's KWKH radio station were heard nationally, as were those of another early radio preacher from Shreveport, Gerald L.K. Smith of the Kings Highway Christian Church. Under Dodd, First Baptist became the nation's first church to own its own radio broadcasting station, located in the church tower built in 1920 when the old church at 515 Travis (built in 1907) was remodeled and enlarged.

Dodd served in numerous offices within the Southern Baptist Convention, including both Louisiana and national president on several occasions. Dodd also traveled the globe on behalf of Baptist missions and became friends with such eminent figures of the day as Mahatma Gandhi; he also authored several books and numerous tracts. While some of the books are collections of his sermons, others describe his travels and today are valuable documents of the world scene between the two great wars, as seen from the perspective of a Shreveport clergyman.

In 1925, Dodd worked to establish a junior college for girls at Shreveport. A year later, Dodd College came into existence. Operating from 1927 to 1942, Dodd College was located in the developing South Highlands area, on Ockley Drive at the foot of Highland Avenue. The same year that Dodd College opened, Dodd left Shreveport to accept the pastorate of a Los Angeles church. Only six months later, however, he returned, becoming president of Dodd College and reassuming the pastorate of First Baptist Church.

A variety of forces led to the closure of Dodd College, among them the Great Depression and the Second World War. In 1943, the campus was sold to Centenary College, which used it as a satellite campus, basing its flight training and ROTC programs there. In 1959, the property came back into the hands of First Baptist Church, which constructed its present church there between 1960 and 1963. The two main buildings of Dodd College are incorporated into today's First Baptist Church and, just down the street at 601 Ockley Drive, the old college president's house, long the home of Dr. and Mrs. Dodd and today the residence of one of his granddaughters and her husband. It is listed on the National Register of Historic Places, chiefly because of its associations with Dodd and Dodd College.

Dr. Dodd was active in city affairs as well as religious. Early in his career here, he championed the closure of the city's legal red-light district, and in 1917 he won that fight. He was also active with the Rotary Club and the chamber of commerce for much of his Shreveport career.

Also during Dodd's pastorate, First Baptist sponsored the establishment of several mission churches throughout the city, all of which are today daughter congregations of First Baptist. Among these are Willow Point Baptist Church (formerly Queensborough Baptist Church), Southside Baptist Church (formerly Cedar Grove Baptist Church), Highland Baptist Church (which recently remerged into First Baptist), New Birth Baptist Church (formerly the Mildred Crowe Memorial Mission), Southern Hills Baptist Church (formerly Allendale Baptist Church), Haynes Avenue Baptist Church (formerly Dixie Garden Baptist Church) and several others.

Following a 1949 heart attack, Dodd decided to retire, effective July 9, 1950. Although retired, he did not become inactive, leaving for Glendale, California, in 1952 to temporarily serve a church there. On August 6, 1952, Dr. Dodd suffered two heart attacks and died in Long Beach, California. His remains were returned to Shreveport and buried at Forest Park Cemetery, where a granite replica of the pulpit of the old downtown First Baptist Church marks his grave.

C.E. Byrd, Influential Area Educator

It can be rightly said that one of the principal founders of the Caddo Parish school system was Professor C.E. Byrd. His legacy is one that has

C.E. Byrd, 1890. *Author's collection.*

brought education to many hundreds of thousands, and although he himself is little remembered today, save in the name of Shreveport's Byrd High School on Line Avenue, a great debt of gratitude is owed him.

In Virginia, where Professor Byrd grew up, the Byrd name was and is a prominent and well-known one, his extended family having produced many notables in that state and indeed the nation's history. Professor Byrd was born on his parents' farm in Bath County, Virginia, on December 14, 1859. He was educated at the Augusta Military Academy and the University of Virginia, after which he was admitted to the Virginia bar as an attorney. The law, however, was not what C.E. Byrd ultimately chose to be his career—education was. Abandoning the legal field almost as soon as he entered it, C.E. Byrd became a teacher and shortly thereafter was made principal of the Fort Royal, Virginia public school. After six years, he accepted a post as principal of the Ouachita Parish High School in faraway Monroe, Louisiana, a position he held for the next three years.

In 1892, Byrd came to Shreveport as principal of the first public high school here, which was then located at the southwest corner of Milam and Edwards Streets. Six years later, the school was moved to temporary quarters on Crockett Street while the new Shreveport Central High School was under construction on Hope Street near Oakland (the present site of the city jail). In 1899, this massive new building, designed in the Romanesque Revival style and featuring a 124-foot-high clock tower at its corner, opened with Byrd as its first principal.

In that same year, Byrd left to serve as city superintendent of schools, remaining in that job until 1908, when he became parish superintendent of schools, a post he held until his death, excepting a year as president of the Louisiana Industrial School at Ruston (later the Louisiana Polytechnic Institute and now Louisiana Tech University).

Though he left Shreveport High School as principal at the end of 1899, Byrd remained close to the school. He was so close, in fact, that it really had two principals during the remainder of Byrd's life—the official principal and Byrd himself. Shreveport High was Byrd's baby and everyone knew it. He set the standards for the school's curriculum, insisting that to be truly educated one had to be familiar with history, math, English and Latin—at the very least! Even while serving as superintendent of schools, Byrd taught geometry, algebra, physics and chemistry classes at the school. He also worked avidly to establish a first-class library for the school, the first public library in Caddo Parish. When Dr. Thomas E. Schumpert, founder of what is now Christus-Schumpert Medical Center, died in 1908, he willed his nearly two-thousand-volume private library to the school, adding immeasurably to Byrd's work.

In 1910, a new Shreveport High was built next door to the old one, which then became a junior high and elementary school. The old Shreveport High School, damaged by fire in 1915 and markedly alerted at that time, stood until 1926, but the newer one remained through the 1970s, serving for many years as the Caddo Vocational-Technical School after its tenure as a high school ended with the construction of two new high schools in the 1920s: New Shreveport High on Line Avenue in 1925 (renamed for Byrd the year after its opening) and Fair Park High on Greenwood Road, built in 1929.

By today's standards, C.E. Byrd was a dichotomy. He vigorously defended the practice of corporal punishment but objected to prayer or school-led devotionals on campus. Byrd argued that corporal punishment was necessary for discipline when all else failed and that school prayer was exclusionary and had no place in a pluralistic society. He himself was a devout Presbyterian but saw no reason to impose his views upon others. In 1912, however, he bent to pressure by fundamentalist groups and reluctantly changed his policies. However, in 1915, the state supreme court declared school prayer unconstitutional in Louisiana, solving the problem. The very case upon which that decision was made, *Herold, et. al. v. Caddo School Board*, was the backbone of the federal school prayer case decided in 1964. Interestingly, the issues that prevail in our schools today are the same ones that did nearly a century ago. Then, as now, they had almost nothing to do with education and everything to do with emotion.

Byrd himself focused on education. He dreamed of seeing several new first-rate schools built in Caddo Parish, and he lived to see the initiation of that dream. Starting in the 1910s, a massive school building program was launched. Most of the schools built at this time still function today. Among these are Hamilton Terrace, Creswell Elementary, Midway Middle School (originally the Jewella School), Fairfield Elementary (originally the Cedar Grove School), Barret Elementary, West Shreveport Elementary, A.C. Steere Elementary (originally the Broadmoor Grammar School), South Highland and Claiborne Elementary, Central Elementary (originally Shreveport Colored High School), Atkins Elementary, the former Hendrix School (originally the Allendale Grammar School), Fair Park High and, of course, C.E. Byrd High. On September 17, 1925, that school was dedicated with Professor Byrd delivering the keynote address. He said that it was the proudest day of his life.

Five months later, on the morning of February 26, 1926, Clifton Ellis Byrd died. His body lay in state in the foyer of the school that bears his name. From there, he was carried to Forest Park Cemetery on St. Vincent Avenue, where he sleeps yet, beside his wife of thirty-two years, Mattie McAfee Byrd, whom he met and married during his time in Monroe. Only a little over a mile away, at the southeast corner of Line and Kings Highway, stands his most visible monument, though the Caddo school system itself is as much his memorial as anything could be.

HEROES AND MOVERS

Bishop Polk, Shreveport's First Clergyman

One of the most interesting figures associated with the early history of Shreveport is Leonidas Polk, Episcopal bishop of Louisiana, a man of national reputation as a clergyman, soldier and scholar. A cousin of U.S. president James Knox Polk and a founder of the University of the South at Sewanee, Tennessee, Bishop Polk conducted what is generally believed to have been the first organized religious service in Shreveport on March 24, 1839, only four days after the little village of Shreve Town was incorporated as the town of Shreveport.

Leonidas Polk was born in Raleigh, North Carolina, on April 10, 1806. He was educated at the University of North Carolina and the United States Military Academy at West Point, class of 1827. In 1828, he married Frances Devereux, daughter of a wealthy sugar planting family of Lafource Parish, Louisiana. That same year, he entered the Virginia Theological Seminary.

In 1830, he was ordained a priest of the Protestant Episcopal Church, and in 1838 he was appointed missionary bishop of the Southern Diocese of the Episcopal Church, with supervision over Arkansas, Louisiana, Mississippi, Alabama, the Indian Territory and the Republic of Texas, a vast territory, to say the least. Four years later, in 1841, he became bishop of the newly created Diocese of Louisiana.

While missionary bishop, the Reverend Polk was active in the organization of Episcopalian congregations throughout Louisiana. In 1839, he came to the then tiny river town of Shreveport to conduct services for the handful

Bishop Leonidas Polk. *Courtesy of St. Mark's Episcopal Cathedral, Shreveport, Louisiana.*

of Episcopalians here. His hope was to organize a congregation in the new community, and ultimately, he was successful.

Bishop Polk came to Shreveport aboard a steamboat called the *Denmark*, which struck a snag and foundered above Shreveport. While the *Denmark* sank, Bishop Polk, who had studied engineering at West Point, assisted in rescuing the passengers and a large portion of the cargo, all of which were transferred to another boat, the *Eradicator*, which continued the journey to Shreveport, arriving here on March 22.

It has often been repeated that Bishop Polk faced bodily harm from those who did not wish him to conduct services here. Certainly, this is a romantic and fanciful account but one without basis in historical evidence. Bishop Polk, who meticulously kept a journal, makes no mention of any problems encountered in conducting services locally. He does say, however, that he addressed "an attentive audience." Furthermore, the newspapers of the day make no mention of any trouble. Indeed, the *Caddo Free Press*, the principal paper in Shreveport in 1839, states:

> *The Rev. Leonidas Polk, of Tennessee, Bishop of the Southern Diocese of the Episcopal Church, performed divine services in this town on Sunday last and delivered an excellent and appropriate discourse to a large and attentive audience. The effects of his visit have been highly beneficial. A desire is generally expressed for the regular observance of religious worship and before long we hope to see a church erected and a suitable individual installed as pastor.*

The story of rowdies and ruffians wanting to prevent the bishop from performing services seems to have been invented years after the fact, indeed years after Polk's death, by his son, who wrote a highly romanticized biography of his father. The younger Polk also claimed that the *Denmark* was raised and brought into port with Polk's aid. The *Denmark*, however, was a complete loss, the remnants of which still lie somewhere on the Red River. The truth of Bishop Polk's accomplishments is far more important and interesting than any legends that have grown up around him.

From that first service grew the foundations of the Episcopal Church in north Louisiana. Still, services were occasional and intermittent until 1845, when some effort to establish an Episcopalian parish was made. Ultimately, it was not until March 1851 that a permanent Episcopal church, first called Grace Church, was established. A month later, the name was changed to St. Mark's Church, today's St. Mark's Cathedral.

In 1858, land for a permanent church building was donated to St. Mark's by Paulina Pickett (services had, up to then, been held at the Caddo Courthouse). Construction began the following year on the building to be located at the northwest corner of Fannin and Market Streets. The church, designed by the noted English architect Frederick Clarke Withers, was completed in 1860 and dedicated by Bishop Polk on April 10, 1861. It would be his last visit to Shreveport.

Shortly after Louisiana seceded from the Union in 1861, Bishop Polk offered his services as a West Point graduate to the army of the Confederate States of America. On June 25, 1861, he was appointed major general of the Provisional Confederate Army. On October 10, 1862, he was commissioned lieutenant general. During the first years of war, he was involved in the fortification of the Mississippi and later served as a corps commander at Shiloh, Perryville, Stones River, Chickamauga and Atlanta.

On June 14, 1864, at Pine Mountain, Georgia, the Right Reverend Leonidas Polk was struck by a cannonball and killed instantly. A monument erected in 1902 marks the spot where he fell. Bishop Polk was buried in St. Paul's Church in Augusta, Georgia, where he remained until 1945, when his remains were reburied, together with those of his widow, next to the high altar of Christ Church Cathedral on St. Charles Avenue in New Orleans.

W.T.D. DALZELL, PHYSICIAN, PRIEST AND HERO

Unquestionably one of the great figures in Shreveport's history is Dr. William Tucker Dickinson Dalzell. A physician and Episcopalian priest, Dalzell achieved nationwide prominence through his work during epidemics of yellow fever. Locally, however, he may be best known by many as the longtime rector of St. Mark's Episcopal Church (now St. Mark's Cathedral).

But who was the Reverend Dr. Dalzell? He was born on the Caribbean island of St. Vincent, in the West Indies, on June 2, 1827, and was educated in medicine in London and at Oxford. Upon becoming a physician, Dalzell took up studies to become a priest. In 1851, he was made a deacon in the Church of England by the bishop of London. A year later, he was ordained a priest by the bishop of Jamaica. He served at Mooretown, Jamaica, briefly in British Guiana (now Guyana) and at Demerara, Venezuela, before coming to the United States.

Dr. Dalzell had contracted and narrowly survived yellow fever during his youth in Jamaica, an event that helped shape his life and his decision to devote his life both to medicine and the church. Left immune to the disease, as are most survivors of yellow fever, Dalzell felt free thereafter to travel into the very midst of communities stricken by that plague where most were fleeing for their lives. Also helping to shape his obsession with yellow fever was the death of his young wife, a daughter of the prominent Urquhart family, who were planters in Jamaica. She perished from the "yellow jack," as it was called, while the couple resided in Venezuela in 1854.

Indeed, it was yellow fever that brought Dalzell to the United States, since that disease was his field of specialty. In 1854, only a short time after

The Reverend Dr. W.T.D. Dalzell (seated) and his wife Estelle. *Author's collection.*

Dr. Dalzell lost his wife to yellow fever in Venezuela, Savannah, Georgia, was attacked by the disease, and physicians with knowledge of the fever were desperately needed. The twenty-seven-year-old Dalzell ventured to Georgia thinking his trip only temporary, but excepting brief trips, he never left the United States again.

In 1855, he went to Philadelphia, becoming rector of the Church of the Ascension. There he married Ellen Underdonk, daughter of the Episcopal bishop of Philadelphia. She became ill, however, and it was supposed that a warmer climate would do her good. Consequently, Dalzell accepted a Houston pulpit, becoming rector of Christ Church. In 1858, Houston, too, experienced an outbreak of yellow fever and Dr. Dalzell remained in the city through the thick of it.

In 1859, he returned with his wife to Philadelphia, where she died in 1860. His reason for leaving Houston had much to do with his opposition to slavery and his difficulties with the vestry of his congregation over his pro-abolition and pro-Union position (this despite his friendship with such eminent southern figures of the day as Robert E. Lee).

Despite his political leanings, Dalzell remained true to his adopted homeland, the South. In 1861, when war broke out, he left Philadelphia and joined the Confederate army, becoming chaplain of a Texas regiment. During part of the war (1862–65), he filled the pulpit of St. Mark's Church in San Antonio. In August 1865, at war's close, he went to New Orleans, where he soon married Miss Estelle Logan of that city.

In April 1866, he accepted the pulpit of St. Mark's Church in Shreveport, and in May he began his pastorate here. In August 1873, he warned the Shreveport Medical Society, of which he was a member, that signs of yellow fever were present and due precaution should be taken. The majority of the medical society criticized Dalzell for being alarmist. Nevertheless, he warned his congregation to leave town at once. Some did but most did not. Within weeks, Shreveport was in the midst of what would go down in history as the third most disastrous outbreak of yellow fever in U.S. history. He stayed in the city and set up several makeshift hospitals. Most of the other members of the Medical Society did not survive.

In 1878, Dalzell went to Memphis to assist that city with its great epidemic, the second most disastrous in U.S. history (the worst was the New Orleans epidemic of 1853). As a hero of Memphis, he accepted a call to that city's Grace Episcopal Church. After two years, however, he returned to Shreveport. His love of the city and the city's love of him (St. Mark's had, after two years, failed to find a new rector) kept Dr. Dalzell here the rest of his life. He even passed up the opportunity to be ordained a bishop so that he might remain in his beloved Shreveport.

He died in Shreveport during the night of February 4–5, 1899. At his funeral the mourners stood in the aisles of St. Mark's Church, which was then located at the northwest corner of Fannin and Market Streets. The building could not accommodate the crowd, and many stood outside, listening through the windows. He was buried at Greenwood Cemetery on Stoner Avenue. Six years later, the new building of St. Mark's on Cotton Street (now home of Holy Cross Episcopal Church) was dedicated "to the glory of God and the memory of Rev. Dr. W.T.D. Dalzell," as its cornerstone reads. About 1914, a Highland-area street was renamed in his memory and honor as well. Dr. Dalzell's onetime home still stands at 758 Austin Place, three doors in from Texas Avenue.

Less than a year after Dr. Dalzell died, the cause of yellow fever's transmission was isolated. The mystery of the disease's transmission had puzzled Dalzell all his life, and he made a serious effort to isolate it. Working independently, U.S. Army physician Walter Reed and Cuban physician Carlos Finlay isolated the carrier as the mosquito. Within a decade of Dalzell's death, yellow fever was not only controlled but virtually eradicated in the United States.

Eugene Woodruff, the Yankee Hero of Shreveport

With the singular exception of the Civil War, the greatest tragedy to directly affect Shreveport was the great yellow fever epidemic of 1873. Nearly a quarter of the town's permanent population was lost thorough death or flight. Even greater was the number of deaths among the nonpermanent population, for in those days Shreveport had a sizeable transient population as well, owing to activity on the river. Shreveport's growth was stunted for years afterward, and it is arguable that the face of the city was forever altered by this one event.

There are hundreds of stories of heroism and tragedy connected with the great epidemic and hundreds more that shall never be known. But among them all, one hero in particular stands out. His name was Eugene

Lieutenant Eugene A. Woodruff. *Author's collection.*

Augustus Woodruff, and he is buried at Oakland Cemetery, where he has lain since his untimely death at the age of thirty-one.

Eugene Woodruff was born November 26, 1841, in Avon, Connecticut. His father died when he was seven, and he and his brother George, as well as two other siblings, were brought up by their mother, Harriette A. Woodruff, who moved the family to Independence, Iowa, in 1857 in order to run a girls' school. During the Civil War, Eugene enlisted in the Union army's Fifth Iowa Volunteer Regiment, Company E, and was elected second corporal. Seven months later, however, Iowa congressman William Vandever informed him that he had received an appointment to West Point. Woodruff entered the U.S. Military Academy in 1862, graduating in 1866, seventh in a class of forty-one.

Woodruff served in the U.S. Army Corps of Engineers first in Missouri and then at Jefferson Barracks in Wisconsin before coming to Louisiana in 1871. He arrived first at New Orleans, where the commanding officer there, Captain Charles W. Howell, assigned him to come to the Shreveport area. He came not as part of the occupying army of the federal government, but rather now as a lieutenant with the U.S. Army Corps of Engineers working to clear the Red River of logs and debris that had re-formed during the three and a half decades since Captain Shreve first made the river navigable.

Much of Woodruff's time was spent on the snagboat *Aid*, along with his brother, George, who was also with the Corps of Engineers. The snagboat was an invention of Captain Shreve: a double-hulled small ship with a large crane mounted between the twin hulls. These boats were used to haul large tree trunks, piles of debris and other "snags" from the river channel. Variations of Shreve's snagboat design were used on American waterways well into the twentieth century.

When in town, Woodruff boarded with the Elstners, a prominent Shreveport family, at their home on the northwest corner of Spring and Fannin Streets. Milton C. Elstner was at the time Shreveport city attorney, and several members of the family figured in local nineteenth-century politics.

In August 1873, a few cases of yellow fever began to appear in Shreveport. Dr. William T.D. Dalzell, rector of St. Mark's Episcopal Church and a physician with experience dealing with the disease, warned the medical community that an epidemic was on the horizon and that every precaution, including possible evacuation of the town, should be taken. The other physicians called Dalzell an alarmist, however, and downplayed the problem until it was too late.

Woodruff, one of Dalzell's congregants, took him seriously. When his superiors learned of the impending epidemic, they ordered all members of the Corps to leave the Shreveport area immediately. Woodruff helped see that they did, but he himself disobeyed the order and stayed behind.

Remaining at the Elstner home, he joined with other Shreveporters who opted not to evacuate the town in nursing the sick and bringing them food. He contacted the Howard Association in New Orleans, a society set up to provide aid in times of epidemics, a very real part of life in nineteenth-century Louisiana, and was instrumental in setting up a chapter of the Howards in Shreveport, bringing in doctors, nurses and medical supplies from New Orleans. He also helped set up a makeshift hospital.

But Woodruff was not among those who were mysteriously immune to the fever, nor was he to be one of those who contracted the disease but survived. On September 23 he fell ill, and on September 30, he died, two months shy of his thirty-second birthday.

Lieutenant Woodruff was laid to rest in the Elstner plot at Oakland Cemetery, where a large monument was placed on his grave. His epitaph reads, "I was sick and you visited me." A month before he died, he wrote to his mother that he would like to marry but had met no young women in Shreveport who appealed to him. He then commented that, in any case, "it would never do for me to stay here." Little did he know that he would never leave.

The *Shreveport Times* printed a lengthy and laudatory obituary for him the day after he died, but his mother would have to fight to receive his pension since he had disobeyed orders in not evacuating the stricken city. Finally, in 1874, a special act of Congress granted her $17 per month for life (about $500 in today's money). She died in 1897. Also in 1874, a U.S. snagboat was christened the *E.A. Woodruff*. It operated on the Ohio River until 1925. George Woodruff succeeded his brother in his duties and finished the job of clearing the river. When Shreveport celebrated its centennial in 1935, George was still alive in Independence, Iowa. Through the *Shreveport Times*, he sent greetings to the people of Shreveport, many of whom were alive because of his brother's selfless heroism and ultimate sacrifice some sixty-two years earlier.

DR. T.E. SCHUMPERT, NAMESAKE OF A MEDICAL CENTER

Sitting atop one of the highest topographical points in the city of Shreveport is one of the region's oldest, largest and best-known medical facilities, Christus-Schumpert Medical Center. Christus-Schumpert, first known as the Shreveport Sanitarium, then as Schumpert Sanitarium and later as Schumpert Hospital, is named for its founder, Dr. Thomas Edgar Schumpert, a pioneer of modern surgery.

Dr. Schumpert was born on October 18, 1861, on his parents' sixteen-hundred-acre plantation near Bethany, Louisiana, just west of Shreveport. He was the only child of Mary Holt Schumpert and Dr. John Ira Schumpert, who was then a surgeon with the Trans-Mississippi Department of the Confederate army. The elder Dr. Schumpert graduated from the School of Physicians and Surgeons in New York City and married in 1859.

T.E. Schumpert received his early education on the plantation but attended the Thatcher Institute, a private military school in Shreveport,

Dr. T.E. Schumpert. *Author's collection.*

for high school. He went on to Louisiana State University and then to the medical college of the University of Louisville, from which he graduated in 1884. For a time after graduation, he did postgraduate work at the New York Polyclinic before returning home to Shreveport, where he became a surgeon at Shreveport Charity Hospital.

In time, Dr. Schumpert became surgeon in charge and chief administrator of the Charity Hospital (later Confederate Memorial Medical Center and today the Louisiana State University Health Sciences Center). In 1896, he attracted international attention by performing the world's first successful ligation of the subclavian artery. That operation took place in the old Charity Hospital building, which stood on the site now occupied by the Shreveport Police and City Court Complex.

About 1892, Schumpert began seeing private patients at his home across Hope Street from the Charity Hospital. In 1894, he established a private clinic there, though he continued to make the Charity Hospital his principal career (his pay there was $75 per month—about $2,000 in today's terms—which the private practice augmented considerably). In 1897, the board of Charity Hospital told him to cease and desist from advertising his clinic in the local newspapers. This he did, but a year later he left Charity altogether and expanded the Schumpert Clinic to become Shreveport Sanitarium.

The new sanitarium's first location was in the building that until recently had been the first home of Shreveport High School, located at the southwest corner of Milam and Edwards Streets and built in 1888 for the YMCA. This facility had only sixteen beds and soon proved inadequate. So, with a grant from the original Louisiana lottery, Schumpert purchased and remodeled a large Victorian building at the northeast corner of Texas Avenue and Grand Avenue, formerly home to the Kate P. Nelson Seminary, a nineteenth-century private girls' school.

The Texas Avenue facility housed the hospital and clinic as well as a nursing school. Schumpert himself oversaw the entire operation until 1904, when the burden of managing the ever-expanding sanitarium became too large for one man to handle. In addition to running the hospital and clinic, Schumpert was also president of the Shreveport Medical Society and the Louisiana State Medical Society and was instrumental in establishing the Tri-State Medical Society, precursor of today's Willis-Knighton Health System. He was also a member of the Shreveport Board of Health and traveled nationally on the lecture circuit, helping to organize and expand medical societies the country over. In 1905, he became city health officer for Shreveport. That same year, he became owner of one of the city's first automobiles, an electric.

Additionally, Schumpert served four area railroads and the streetcar system as their contract surgeon and also worked as medical examiner for several insurance companies. He was a member of the board of the State Fair of Louisiana and was a director of Commercial National Bank. He was also the owner of extensive real estate holdings. Indeed, by 1907, his outside activities, coupled with stress and declining health, led Schumpert, a devout Catholic (though he had been raised Lutheran), to invite the Sisters of Charity of the Incarnate Word, from Houston, to assume control of the hospital.

On May 16, 1908, T.E. Schumpert succumbed to typhoid in his own hospital; he was five months short of his forty-seventh birthday. He was buried at Greenwood Cemetery in a stately mausoleum next to his mother, who had died in 1893. His father would join them there in 1912. T.E. Schumpert never married.

In 1909, the sisters—to whom Schumpert had willed the sanitarium—purchased a ten-acre lot on Margaret Place in the developing Highland area. The Margaret Place property was formerly the site of Fort Jenkins during the Civil War. In 1911, the T.E. Schumpert Memorial Sanitarium opened there and has been there ever since.

Over the decades, the hospital has grown and expanded many times. In 1957, the old, four-story, red brick building with its columned portico of the Doric order and its wide sleeping porches was replaced by a ten-story, 342-bed facility. It, in turn, has been enlarged several times since to almost three times its 1957 size, becoming the medical center we know today. Although a small street in Ledbetter Heights honors Dr. Schumpert, his real monument is the medical center that he founded which bears his name, a fitting memorial to an important leader in his field and city.

Adah DeLay, the Christmas Tree Lady

In Oakland Cemetery, beneath the shady trees that give the oldest burial ground in Shreveport its name, stands a new monument. It was quietly placed there in 1997 by the United Daughters of the Confederacy (UDC), even though the person buried beneath died almost sixty-four years earlier.

The recipient of this fine granite marker was not a soldier of the Confederacy but rather a woman born fifteen years after the end of the War Between the States, a woman whose husband was a Northerner and whose philanthropic work for some of Shreveport's neediest and smallest citizens was almost forgotten after she died. Adah Vinson DeLay was that woman's name.

Adah Vinson DeLay was the daughter of Shreveport mayor Richard Tucker Vinson, an early graduate of Centenary College, a Bossier Parish planter and a captain in the Confederate army. Her mother was the former Sarah "Sallie" Hill of Shreveport. Adah was a charter member of the Shreveport Chapter No. 237 of the UDC, a member of St. Mark's Episcopal Church and an active member of the Oakland Cemetery Association, which once existed to maintain and beautify Oakland Cemetery.

Adah Vinson DeLay and one of her orphan charges, circa 1930. *Author's collection.*

In 1900, she married Cyril Scott DeLay, a Wisconsin native who had come to Shreveport after being hired as managing editor of the *Shreveport Times*. Only two years and two months after their marriage, Cyril suddenly died, leaving Adah a widow. He was twenty-seven years old, she twenty-two.

Despite her extreme youth when widowed, Adah never remarried, and though she never gave birth to children of her own she could hardly have been called childless for long. While still in her twenties, she became involved with charity work on behalf of sick children. In 1912, she was given charge of the baby ward of Charity Hospital (later Confederate Hospital and now the LSU Health Sciences Center), where she had worked for some time with the St. Mark's Hospital Guild, sewing blankets and linens and providing entertainment for the children. Under Adah's charge, the baby ward was first equipped with an incubator, wheelchairs and other furnishings. If a child in the ward died, Adah saw to it that a proper burial was made, never allowing any infant to be buried in a pauper's grave, even if she had to pay for the funeral out of her own pocket.

While working at Charity Hospital, Adah began a tradition of providing a Christmas tree for the children and giving a present to each. She even persuaded interns to dress up as Santa Claus to provide the gifts. Because of this gesture, she became known affectionately as "the Christmas Tree Lady," a title she accepted with graciousness.

In addition to her hospital work, Adah Vinson DeLay personally chaired the Oakland Cemetery Association several times and for over twenty years oversaw the cemetery's upkeep. Additionally, she played a role in the erection both of the Confederate Monument on the courthouse lawn and the Confederate Monument at Oakland Cemetery. As long as she lived, she saw to it that flags were placed on the graves of both Confederate and Union soldiers at Oakland on the appropriate memorial days.

But Adah Vinson DeLay's greatest service was found in her work with orphaned children. In the early 1900s, although two orphanages operated privately within the city, Shreveport had no adoption agencies and no mechanism for placing orphaned or unwanted children in proper homes. Consequently, Adah worked to see that void filled, often taking children into her own home until arrangements with adoptive families could be made. During her lifetime, she is known to have facilitated the placement of over two thousand children in the Shreveport area, thoroughly screening all applicants by insisting upon references from clergy and physicians and insisting upon proof of marriage and homeownership. Each placement was done with the prospective parents paying legal filing fees, and in every case Adah accompanied them to the lawyer's office.

Additionally, Adah took in young women and girls who were unmarried and pregnant. If the women wished, Adah would mediate the adoption of their children. Otherwise, she helped them find jobs and homes. Her own home became a haven for young women who were victims of abuse as well, long before shelters for battered women came to be.

Although from a wealthy family, Adah DeLay was nearly penniless when she died in 1933 at the age of only fifty-three. In three decades of charity and philanthropic work, she had expended nearly all of her considerable savings and investments. Just before Christmas 1933, she fell ill with pneumonia at her Merrick Street home. After a week's hospitalization, she died on December 21. Both local newspapers carried the story of her death under bold front-page headlines. She was buried in her family's plot at Oakland Cemetery, next to her parents and husband, but there was no money left for a monument.

It was the late Jane Newberry, a Shreveport schoolteacher, UDC member and an expert on the history of Oakland Cemetery, who researched the location of Adah's grave and became determined that a marker needed to be placed there. Central Monument Company, together with the local UDC chapter and historian Katherine Brash Jeter, donated the marker, which bears an epitaph composed by Mrs. Newberry and this author. The stone now marks the grave of one of Shreveport's most generous and yet unsung personalities. The world could use more people like Adah Vinson DeLay today.

AFTER THE MONKEY TRIAL: JOHN THOMAS SCOPES OF SHREVEPORT

The name John Thomas Scopes is synonymous with one of the most public trials in the history of American jurisprudence. Variously known as "the Scopes trial," "the monkey trial" and "the trial of the century," the real defendant in the case was less Scopes himself than the theory of evolution, which he was convicted of teaching to students in Dayton, Tennessee.

John Thomas Scopes, November 1968. *Photograph by Lloyd Stilley. Author's collection.*

The Scopes trial started out as a contrived publicity stunt hatched by several town fathers in Dayton in order to bring attention to their sleepy and stagnating community. Scopes volunteered to be the defendant in a test case that would challenge a Tennessee statute that prohibited the teaching of any theory of creation aside from that of the Biblical one. Ultimately, though, the trial would pit progressive thought against fundamentalism and secularism against spiritualism. It would also pit two of the great legal minds of their age, Clarence Darrow and William Jennings Bryan, against one another. It was the first trial to be exhaustively covered by the national media and the first to be broadcast via radio around the world. Ultimately, it would kill Bryan, a former secretary of state and thrice presidential candidate. What he saw as a battle for the soul of Christendom was to be his last, for he would die in Dayton just days after the trial's finish.

For his "crime," Scopes was fined $100, though the verdict was later reversed on technical grounds. Despite losing, however, Scopes helped significantly to pave the way for the teaching of the theory of evolution in the public schools not only of Tennessee (where the Butler Act was not repealed until 1967) but also throughout the nation. Scopes himself referred to the outcome as "a victorious defeat."

But what of the young schoolteacher Scopes? What became of him after disappearing from view even at his own trial? Aside from the highly fictionalized movie *Inherit the Wind* and its remake, Scopes receded into relative obscurity. After the trial, despite lucrative offers to capitalize on his newfound fame, he quit teaching, entered graduate school at the University of Chicago to study geology, took a position with Gulf Oil Company and moved briefly to Venezuela, where he met his wife, Mildred. Then, in 1933, eight years after the landmark trial that bears his name ended, Scopes took a job with United Gas and moved to Shreveport, where he would reside for the rest of his life, dying here on October 21, 1970, at the age of seventy.

Commenting in 1960, when he returned briefly to Dayton for the premiere of *Inherit the Wind*, Scopes described the trial's ultimate outcome as "victorious in two respects: Religious freedom—that came in the Constitution; and academic freedom—a new concept of academic freedom that spread throughout the universities and colleges of America…both essential freedoms."

Darrow, Scopes's attorney and one of the most outspoken figures of the first half of the century, said of Scopes that "he is here [on trial] because ignorance and bigotry are rampant, and it is a mighty combination." H.L. Mencken, the colorful Baltimore journalist and another outspoken figure of the early twentieth century, related to his readers the story of a gorilla that had been brought to Dayton as part of the circuslike atmosphere that surrounded the event. Mencken described the ape as "cowering in the corner of his cage, afraid that he might, in fact, be somehow related to the yokels on the opposite side of the bars."

To this day, there persist those who insist on continuing to fight over theories such as evolution, the big bang and so forth; little has changed in the years since the Scopes trial. John Thomas Scopes made a significant contribution to the evolution of American society, education and religion, whether he realized it at the trial's end. His was a battle waged not on behalf of Darwin or of Darwin's theory so much as it was on behalf of freedom of thought. As Scopes himself later said, "Freedom is something that society must fight for and always guard. If you lose one, you lose more. One infringement on the rights of people leads to other infringements. Eventually, the right is destroyed."

Scopes was a quiet freedom fighter. After returning to the United States, he settled down to raise a family in Shreveport's then newly developing Broadmoor area. The Scopes family addresses were 297 (now 295) Carrolton until 1948, 155 Pennsylvania from 1948 to 1957 and 2934 Moss Point Drive on Cross Lake from 1957 until his death in 1970. So little did he discuss his past that one day his son, John Jr., phoned him from college, explaining that the subject of "the monkey trial" had come up in class and that he had ended up being put on the spot. Never having heard of the event, he asked his father, "What the devil are they talking about?"

Both of Scopes's sons, Johnny and William, followed in their father's footsteps. After graduating from Jesuit High School—the Scopeses were deeply committed and active members of the Roman Catholic Church—the sons both entered the oil and gas business, going to work for Texas Eastern Transmission Corporation and United Gas Pipeline Corporation. William C. Scopes later became an independent petroleum land man.

From a short time after her husband's death and until her own in 1983, Scopes's widow lived in the Parkway Apartments in the Madison Park area of Shreveport. They are buried in the Scopes family lot at Oak Haven Cemetery in Paducah, Kentucky, the city where John T. Scopes was born on August 3, 1900. Some might call Paducah John's hometown despite the fact that he resided there for only his first twenty years; but he resided in Shreveport for thirty-seven years, far longer than in any other place. In truth, Shreveport was the city John Thomas Scopes called his hometown. Here he found peace and a respite from the fame and also the notoriety that haunted him throughout his adult life; here he raised his family; here he built his career; and here, in Shreveport, he became a respected part of the community, his church and the oil and gas business.

Ironically, although Scopes was always a retiring man who shunned celebrity, his name is remembered the world over as that of a progressive who helped change the face of his society and his age. On his gravestone is the simple epitaph that summarizes his life: "A Man of Courage."

WILLIS BUTLER, PIONEERING FORENSIC EXAMINER

One of the single most interesting figures in Shreveport's history was longtime Caddo Parish coroner Willis P. Butler, MD, a medical examiner for six decades. When he died at the ripe old age of 103 in June 1991, Dr. Butler was the oldest former medical examiner in the world.

Willis Butler was born at Gibsland, in Bienville Parish, in 1888. He received his undergraduate degree from Vanderbilt University in Nashville and pursued postgraduate studies at Columbia and Cornell Universities in New York City and Ithaca, New York, respectively. He also did postgraduate work at Bellevue Hospital in New York City.

In 1912, Dr. Butler became Caddo Parish coroner, replacing Dr. Arthur A. Herold, who had left that position a year earlier. Dr. Butler remained coroner continuously until his first retirement in 1961. It was a short-lived retirement, however, for in 1962 Butler returned to the job, though in 1966 he was succeeded by Stuart DeLee. In 1974, Dr. Butler was again called out of retirement, serving as Caddo coroner until 1979, when he finally called an end to his long career, moving to Nashville, Tennessee, where he died twelve years later.

Willis Butler was a pioneer in his field. As the late Dr. George McCormick, Caddo Parish coroner until his sudden death in late 2005, said in a 1988 interview about Dr. Butler: "He was seventy-five years ahead of his time. At the time he was in his glory, Shreveport was the mecca of forensic pathology." And if Shreveport was the mecca of forensic pathology, it was because of Willis Butler, a true progressive who was, indeed, ahead of his—or even, in some respects, the present—time.

From 1919 to 1923, Butler ran the Shreveport Morphine Maintenance Clinic, an early attempt to treat morphine, opium and laudanum addicts, who accounted for the majority of drug addicts in that period (and it was a widespread problem even then). Butler viewed drug addicts as physically ill persons rather than criminals, a view then, as now, not shared by law enforcement authorities. In 1923, the

Dr. Willis P. Butler. *Photograph by Langston McEachern, circa 1965. Author's collection.*

authorities shut down the clinic, which distributed measured doses of the drugs to addicts in order to keep them from committing criminal acts to support their addictions. As with the present era's "war on drugs," the actions of lawmakers and law enforcers only led to an increase in crime rather than a decrease in addiction (which increased also and continues to do so). Ultimately, however, the Morphine Maintenance Clinics of Dr. Butler were used as the model for later methadone clinics, which initially (and when adequately funded and operated) met with substantial success.

Another innovation of Dr. Butler's was the use of death masks, an early forerunner to modern facial reconstruction techniques. Additionally, the fact that Caddo Parish's coroner was a trained and certified pathologist was almost unique in the country at the time Dr. Butler began performing autopsies in 1916. Today we should expect that to be the case, but amazingly, even now a medical degree is not a requirement for the position of parish medical examiner in Caddo.

In 1963, Dr. Butler published a book of his memoirs as Caddo Parish coroner. It is entitled *Will Somebody Call the Coroner?* and was published by Vantage Press of New York. As odd as it seems, considering its rather morbid subject matter, Butler's book is a most enjoyable read. *Will Somebody Call the Coroner?* is the story of a bit of Shreveport's history that would certainly not have been recorded for public consumption without a man like Willis P. Butler to do it. Between its covers lies a number of stories ranging from amusing to frightening, to hilariously funny, to utterly bizarre: stories of mistaken identities, missing persons who turn up eventually after having been declared dead and cultural clashes and misunderstandings in a racially segregated society that was poised on the brink of explosive change. It is a story of a doctor who went to work in a horse-drawn buggy in his early years in office, made arrests for murders he investigated, held off lynch mobs at the courthouse on Texas Street and came perilously close to being killed himself on several occasions. If there is anything to complain about in Butler's book, it is the fact that its chapters are very short and the reader is left always wanting more.

Butler's book is immortality in print for its author. His pioneering efforts in the fields of forensics and drug dependency treatment have guaranteed him a place in the annals of American medicine. Willis P. Butler, MD, was truly a Shreveport legend whose career began when the airplane was a new invention and ended when the personal computer was becoming commonplace. His was a remarkable legacy and he a remarkable man. Shreveport is today a major center of medical science due in part to his important groundwork.

BUSINESS LEADERS

Edward Jacobs, Early Merchant and Banker

Few Shreveport businessmen exerted as much influence upon the growth of the city's early economy as did Edward Jacobs, a man whose name was prominent in the city's history. Known to his many friends simply as Ed Jacobs, he was born Ephraim Jacobi in Freienwalde, Pomerania, Germany, on April 9, 1822. At sixteen, he was apprenticed to a tanner in the town of Uckermunde but grew restless and left after two months, traveling around Germany and through Europe doing odd jobs in various cities, eventually landing in the Italian city of Trieste, then under Austrian control. In Trieste, he obtained a passport from the Prussian Consulate and embarked for America, clueless as to where he was headed.

Jacobi's ship, the *Richmond*, landed in Mobile, Alabama, on January 10, 1842, after a ten-week crossing. He had earned his way across the Atlantic working as a crew member aboard the ship, and upon reaching Mobile he was offered further employment by the captain but declined.

Later in January, young Ephraim headed to New Orleans. There he anglicized his name to Edward Jacobs, purchased a small stock of general merchandise on credit and went into business in the suburb of Carrollton. After a time, he decided to head north, into the little-known part of Louisiana watered by the Red River. There was substantial demand for provisions of all sorts in north Louisiana yet relatively few providers of such. Peddlers who went from farm to farm were doing a brisk business; in 1843, Jacobs joined their ranks.

Edward Jacobs. *Author's collection.*

Early in 1844, Ed Jacobs's travels brought him to Shreveport, a new town of fewer than one thousand inhabitants that had been founded only eight years before. Here he decided to settle. Setting up a general merchandise store on the levee (today's Commerce Street), he soon was doing so well that he needed help running the place. He wrote home to Prussia, asking for his younger brother, Benjamin, to come and join him at Shreveport, which he did that same year. Jacobs's business was known as E.&B. Jacobs and Company and sold just about everything from household goods to clothing to groceries, guns, tobacco, liquors and hardware. Within a decade, it was the largest such business in the city, and by the time of the Civil War it occupied a large three-story building on Texas Street. Ed Jacobs was also a cotton factor, a dealer in hides and furs and the owner of considerable rental property, including warehouses along the riverfront that could be leased for the storage of goods being transferred to and from market by river.

In 1850, Ed Jacobs married Palestine Cole, daughter of a local planter. Ultimately, they would have twelve children together. Benjamin later married Palestine's sister, Amazon. When the Civil War broke out, Jacobs played a crucial role in developing Shreveport's wartime economy. Acting as an agent for the Confederate government after the fall of New Orleans in the spring of 1862, he helped move millions of dollars' worth of livestock and cotton from the Confederate interior to Mexico, via Texas. These goods passed through Shreveport, which thus became a vital hub of the Confederacy. From here they were transferred to Mexico and then to Europe. In exchange, ammunition and gold passed through Shreveport and on into the interior of the South the same way.

At the time the Civil War broke out, Ed Jacobs, until then cleanshaven, vowed not to shave or trim his beard again until the war had ended in a Confederate victory. When he died thirty-five years later with no such victory having been achieved, his beard was unquestionably his most recognizable feature, though he does appear to have trimmed it ever so slightly on occasion, to judge from various photographs of him in later life.

Jacobs's wartime efforts earned him a reputation as a financier, and in 1877, he put his brother in charge of the store and established a bank. In 1880, he sold out entirely to his brother, devoting all his energies to the bank. His son, Walter Byron Jacobs, joined him in the banking operation, which became known as the Banking House of E.&W.B. Jacobs.

In 1884, Ed and Walter established a large cotton compress, located on Lake Street. Both owned cotton-producing land, and for a time following the Civil War, Jacobs had also engaged in the cattle business in Texas. On December 3, 1886, the Jacobs Bank was chartered as the First National Bank of Shreveport, with Ed as president and Walter as cashier. During Ed's lifetime, the bank grew to be the largest in Louisiana outside of New Orleans.

Jacobs also was instrumental, along with other prominent investors, including Peter Youree, in developing the Shreveport Street Railways Company, the city's first transit system. His grandson would run that company for many years. In 1890, Shreveport became the first city in the state to have electric streetcars, three years ahead of New Orleans.

The Jacobs family home was one of the city's finest, an enormous Queen Anne Victorian mansion that stood at the southwest corner of Travis and McNeill Streets. Built as a simple two-story house by former mayor R.N. Wood in the late 1840s, it was purchased by the Jacobs family about 1850 and was extensively enlarged and remodeled in 1886. The Jacobs mansion stood until 1923, when it was donated by the Jacobs heirs to the YMCA, which demolished it to make way for the organization's present Shreveport headquarters.

Ed Jacobs died on January 12, 1896, and was buried in the family plot at Oakland Cemetery, located on the edge of the Jewish section but just outside it. In this way, Ed Jacobs, a founding member of the Har El Synagogue in 1859 (now B'nai Zion Temple), could be buried with his Baptist wife yet still be close to the Jewish cemetery. Later biographical sketches would attempt to conceal Jacobs's Jewish origins, something he himself never did. It was his brother Ben who gave the land for Hebrew Rest Cemetery on Texas Avenue in 1886, though he, too, is buried in the nonsectarian part of Oakland.

The First National Bank remained a strong Shreveport institution until the oil bust of the 1980s, which did so much damage to the city's petroleum-dependent economy at the time. The bank became, through a series of mergers and acquisitions, part of the Premier Bank system, itself acquired in turn by Bank One and it, in turn, by Chase Bank. First National's first home, as well as that of the earlier Jacobs Bank, still stands and is now the Spring Street Historical Museum.

Mrs. Jacobs lived until 1918. She was instrumental in establishing the old Genevieve Orphanage in 1889, together with Dr. W.S. Penick, pastor of the First Baptist Church and father-in-law of one of the Jacobses' daughters. Dr. Penick eulogized Ed Jacobs after his death in 1896, calling him "my best friend" and "the greatest man I ever knew." The city of Shreveport honored him by naming a street running between Fairfield and Southern Avenues Jacobs Street, an honor he lived to see.

Emanuel Phelps, More Than a Cobbler

"Phelps Shoes Are Good Shoes." This was the slogan of one of Shreveport's longest operating and most respected businesses, the Phelps Shoe Company, which was founded in 1869 and continued in operation until its final liquidation 116 years later, in 1985. The story of Phelps Shoes is a fascinating segment of Shreveport history, for although the company has been gone for some time now, its influence was tremendous.

Emanuel Phelps. *Author's collection.*

The original Phelps of Phelps Shoes was Emanuel Phelps, a German Jewish shoemaker who came to the United States in 1854 when only fourteen years old. Landing in New York, young Emanuel made his way to Mississippi, where his brother had established a store. There Emanuel went to work as a peddler, traveling from farm to farm and from plantation to plantation selling a variety of goods, particularly leather goods and shoes, which he made and repaired. He also entertained his customers with his musical abilities.

In time, Phelps saved enough money to start his own shoe business in New Orleans, setting up shop on Poydras Street. In New Orleans, he met a teenage English-born girl named Fannie Wolfe. The two married, but soon thereafter the Civil War broke out. Emanuel enlisted in the Confederate army but never saw active service. Almost immediately after his enlistment, New Orleans was taken by Federal forces, and after the war's end, the bank from which Phelps had borrowed the money to start his store failed. By the late 1860s, Phelps was almost completely wiped out financially.

In May 1869, having been unsuccessful in reversing their fortunes in New Orleans, the Phelpses moved to Shreveport. Here Emanuel started a new store, one that would make him a wealthy man and would spread his, and Shreveport's, fame the nation over.

In the 1860s and 1870s, there was great demand for "bench-made" shoes and boots and Phelps specialized in custom-made footwear for his clients, creating made-to-order shoes and boots for men, women and children. He also carried a large assortment of gentlemen's hats and ladies' hosiery.

Most of the shoes and boots sold by Phelps were not custom made, however, but were sold off the rack. These were cheaper than custom-made shoes and boots but not nearly so comfortable, as custom-made footwear was formed to the size and shape of the foot of the individual purchaser. For footwear purchased off the rack, there was no differentiation between shoes for the left and right foot. Like socks today, each unit in a pair of shoes or boots was identical to the other and could be worn on either foot interchangeably. The soft leather or cloth (in the case of some ladies' shoes) simply formed to the shape of the foot over time. Not until the turn of the twentieth century did formfitting shoes become the norm for non-custommade footwear. Nor were separate sizes common; shoes came typically in three sizes: small, medium and large, and two widths: wide and narrow.

Female footwear customers in the nineteenth century did not try on shoes in the store but had multiple pairs delivered to their homes. To try on shoes in the store would be scandalous, since male employees would see the ankle or a bit of leg, and that would never do. The shoes delivered would come tied together by their laces; shoe boxes were unknown in those days. Sometimes a dozen pairs would be sent to a lady's home and eleven of the dozen would return. Other times, all twelve pairs would return together with instructions to custom make a shoe in the style of one or more of the pairs. These instructions would be accompanied by measurements of the foot to be fitted. With ladies' shoes, even custom fitting often involved a good deal of guesswork in those days. Not until after the First World War did it become commonplace for women to try on shoes in the store, about the same time that arching and styling in the modern manner began to come into vogue, with lighter-weight shoes replacing the high-buttoned boots of an earlier era.

Correct shoe fitting was a novel concept when Emanuel Phelps introduced it as a feature of his store in the late nineteenth century. No shoemaker or seller in Shreveport had ever offered such a service, nor had many anywhere in the nation outside of major cities (and few had there). This particular innovation, now so common that it is hard to imagine a time when it was not, was the ultimate key to the Phelps Company's great success.

For many years, Phelps Shoes maintained a collection of examples of shoes made and sold by the firm from its earliest days up until World War II. The whereabouts of this collection today are unknown, which is a shame since this would be truly fascinating today.

After the move to Shreveport from New Orleans, Fannie Phelps gave birth to the couple's three children, but sadly, she would not live to see them grow up or to see her husband become a pillar of the community. In January 1875, she died at the age of twenty-nine.

Phelps married again, this time to Julia Brooks, a native of Niagara Falls, New York. They resided at the small frame home Phelps had purchased at 309 Edwards Street in 1876, and here Julia gave birth to a son and a daughter. In 1897, the old house was moved to the back of the property, and a spacious new house was built by the Phelpses on its site, the finished product being one of the city's finest Victorian-style homes. In 1906, Julia died here, leaving Emanuel widowed for the second time.

In 1875, the same year Fannie had died, Emanuel's nephew, Bernard Sokoloski, joined the firm as its first hired employee (by the mid-1930s, there were twenty-eight). In 1906, Bernard bought into the company as an equal partner with his uncle and cousin, Ben Phelps Sr., Emanuel and Fannie's son. Bernard would remain with the store until his death in 1945 and Ben until his in 1962. Phelps's other son, Ephraim, worked in the business for a time but later moved to Miami, Florida. He died in 1960, still a part owner of the firm.

Through the years, the company's size and reputation grew. First located at 203 Texas Street, it moved across the street to 216 in the 1880s. In 1912, the company moved to 412 Texas Street, and in 1970 to 509 Market Street. The latter address, in the Lane Building, remained open through the remainder of the store's history. Two other locations opened in the 1970s as well, at Pierremont Mall and Shreve City Shopping Center.

But the Phelps Shoe Company's sales were not limited strictly to the Shreveport area. By the 1920s, the firm was already shipping to all parts of the nation and even abroad, both to individual customers and to shoe stores. A 1939 customer list shows clients in Hawaii, South America, Egypt, countries throughout Europe and cities all across the United States.

Emanuel Phelps lived until 1931, when, at age ninety, he, like Julia a quarter century earlier, died at the big house on Edwards Street. The house then became the residence of his and Julia's daughter and son-in-law, Anita and Martin Kirsch. It stood until 1949, when the Kirsches moved to Broadmoor and sold the old mansion for commercial development. One of their children, Emanuel Phelps Kirsch, later became famous as a painter and interior designer, working in Paris and New York under the pseudonym Jean-Pierre Pique (pronounced "P.K." for "Phelps Kirsch," a pseudonym formula he adopted from his mentor and friend, the artist-designer Erté, whose own pseudonym is the French pronunciation of the initials of his birth name, Romain de Tirtiff).

Emanuel Phelps rests at Hebrew Rest Cemetery on Texas Avenue; Julia lies beside him. Fannie lies in the old Jewish section of Oakland Cemetery off Sprague Street. During the sixty-two years that Emanuel Phelps spent in Shreveport, he was an active and important part of the city, a member of the chamber of commerce from its inception in 1910 and a leader in many other civic organizations. But it was Phelps's pioneering ideas about how shoes should be made and sold that made his name a household phrase the nation over and even abroad and made his slogan, "Phelps Shoes are Good Shoes," an example of truth in advertising.

Captain Peter Youree, Father of Modern Shreveport

Youree Drive is one of Shreveport's most important roads and is unquestionably the main thoroughfare of southeast Shreveport. From its beginnings near downtown at the convergence of Spring and Market, just south of the central business district, it runs south for several miles, eventually becoming known simply as Highway One South. It is appropriate that such an important street should be named Youree Drive, for Peter Youree was one of the creators of modern Shreveport. His is one of the city's most familiar names, yet many today are not certain just who he was.

Peter Youree was born on April 23, 1843, in Lafayette County, Missouri. Just before his eighteenth birthday, he enlisted in the Confederate army, joining Company A of Shelby's Missouri Cavalry. During the course of the war, he attained the rank of captain, fighting in several battles in Missouri as well as with the Army of Tennessee. His last wartime service was as captain of Company I, Slayback's Regiment of Missouri Rifles.

By war's end, Youree was penniless, having been paid in what was by then worthless scrip. Honorably discharged at Shreveport, he decided to remain here. After all, having joined up at seventeen, he left behind no wife or career in Missouri, and without funds, there seemed even less reason to return. So twenty-two-year-old Pete Youree, as he was known to friends, took a job as a clerk for a modest wage. Such was the foundation of one of Shreveport's important careers.

As time went by, Youree began to acquire property. In 1877, he bought the Shreveport Street Railway, a nearly defunct streetcar system begun in 1870. Reorganizing the company and taking on partners, Youree built the basis for Shreveport's present-day transit system. In 1890, under his direction, Shreveport became the first city in Louisiana to inaugurate electric streetcar service (previously, mules had been used to pull the streetcars). The system was expanded many times over the years, experiencing great growth under the direction of Youree and his successors, especially the Jacobs brothers early in this century. In 1939, the

Peter Youree. *Author's collection.*

electric cars were replaced by trolleys and, still later, by today's city buses. What started out as a private venture under Pete Youree is now the metro area's public transit authority, Sportran.

In 1888, Youree became president of the Merchants and Farmers Bank, located in the building at Texas and Spring that now houses the Blind Tiger Restaurant. In 1891, he sold his interests in that bank and became vice-president of Commercial National Bank, established in 1886. Upon the death of CNB's president, Captain Simon Levy, in 1898, Youree took over the bank's reins. He would hold that position until his death sixteen years later.

In 1910, CNB began to realize Peter Youree's dream, the erection of a ten-story headquarters. The new building, one of the tallest in the state at the time, was completed in 1911 and was Shreveport's first building over five stories in height. The bank moved from its old building, an elegant red brick Victorian structure designed by local architect N.S. Allen, to the new "skyscraper" at Texas and Market. Youree's ten-story skyscraper still stands at 509 Market Street, today dwarfed by its surrounding neighbors, but the older bank building with its mansard roof, located at the northeast corner of Milam and Market, was demolished in the early 1980s.

In 1910, Peter Youree built the city's largest, grandest and most modern hotel of the day at the southwest corner of Market and Travis Streets. Called the Hotel Youree, it was later (1923) joined to the Washington Hotel, another grand hotel just to its rear, facing Edwards Street. Thus was born the famous old Washington-Youree, for decades one of Shreveport's true landmarks. In time, the hotel was again split into two entities, with the old Washington side retaining the Washington-Youree name while the old Youree side came to be called the Captain Shreve; both were demolished in December 1979 and January 1980.

Additionally, Youree was among those instrumental in building the city's first waterworks, the McNeill Pumping Station, in 1887. For years he served as president of the waterworks company, originally a private venture, though the genesis of today's public water and sewerage utility. He was also a member and president of the Caddo Parish Police Jury (forerunner to today's Caddo Commission) and was responsible for many of the parish's early road-paving projects. Despite being the single largest taxpayer in the parish at the time, Youree proposed the levying of a road tax for the purpose of paving parish highways, including—even especially—Highway One.

Pete Youree married Mary Elizabeth Scott of Scottsville, Texas, near Marshall, in 1870. They had two children, William Scott Youree (1872–1904) and Susan Rose Youree (1881–1974), later wife of A.T. Lloyd of Dallas, Texas. The Youree home, Youreeka, stood at 1525 Fairfield. Initially a sprawling Victorian home designed by N.S. Allen, the house was extensively remodeled at the turn of the century, resulting in the Greek Revival mansion that many older Shreveporters remember. In 1939, shortly after Mrs. Youree's death, Youreeka was demolished to build the United Gas Building, now the State Office Building. Much of the grounds surrounding that building, as well as the fence, are remnants of Youreeka's park.

On July 31, 1914, after having suffered a long illness, Peter Youree died. Although he donated the Confederate Monument at Shreveport's Greenwood Cemetery, he was not buried there. Nor indeed was he even buried in Shreveport. Instead he rests in Scottsville, Texas, near his wife, children and many of their relatives. The lovely little chapel there was built by the Yourees in memory of their son, and they all rest in its shadow.

It is said that Peter Youree was the first to use the term "Greater Shreveport" in describing his vision of the city's future as an important metropolitan area. Although not a native, Youree's impact on Shreveport was profound. He helped to bring the city into the twentieth century after all. It is only fitting that an important road should be named for him, though that is by no means his only memorial here. The modern city itself, Greater Shreveport, is in many very real respects a monument to the life and work of Peter Youree.

M.T. Hancock, Tragic Inventor

One of the most curious memorials at Greenwood Cemetery on Stoner Avenue is the large stone tomb of Milton Taylor Hancock. Located near the center of the older half of the cemetery, not far from the main gate, the Hancock tomb is particularly conspicuous because of its rusted iron doors and austere appearance. Over the years, lots of stories have arisen about this tomb and the people buried within, though little has been actually documented. Here, however, is the story of the Hancocks and their peculiar tomb.

Tomb of Colonel Milton Taylor Hancock, Greenwood Cemetery, Shreveport, Louisiana. *Photo by author.*

Milton Taylor Hancock was born in 1858. He grew up in Indiana and came to Shreveport as a traveling salesman while still a very young man, marrying and attaining a good deal of attention as an amateur inventor. In the early 1890s, he experimented with the idea of a rotary disk plow. Earlier attempts by others at making disk plows had failed, but Colonel Hancock, as he was known, kept at it, trying different styles and materials and persisting in his endeavor despite the skepticism of others.

Not all were skeptical, however. Among his supporters was Senator Thomas C. Barret, later to be Louisiana's lieutenant governor, who assisted Hancock in achieving a patent for his device in 1893. That same year, the Hancock Plow Company was chartered in Shreveport as a public corporation with an initial capital stock of $100,000. The first board included Senator Barret; his brother-in-law, and later Louisiana governor, Newton Crain Blanchard; cotton factor and merchant W.F. Taylor; planters James M. Foster and J.M. Hollingsworth; and Colonel Hancock.

The ultimate success of Colonel Hancock's rotary disk plow was sealed in 1894 when it beat the top-selling moldboard and land-slide plow of Parlin and Orendorf, then the largest plow manufacturer in America, in a contest waged in McKinney, Texas. Hancock took the $500 prize and more publicity than any amount of money could have purchased.

By 1898, the manufacture and marketing of the Hancock plow was well underway. By 1900, it had become the highest-selling plow on the American market, not an insignificant achievement in a nation that still had a largely agrarian economy. Factories producing the plow were set up in Indianapolis, Indiana; Chattanooga, Tennessee; San Francisco, California; Kansas City, Missouri; Springfield, Illinois; Atlanta, Georgia; Montgomery, Alabama; New Orleans, Louisiana; and Marshall, Texas. Why no factory was established in Shreveport, Hancock's city of residence, is unclear.

In any case, by 1899, at the age of forty-one, Milton T. Hancock was a millionaire. But all was not necessarily rosy for Hancock and his wife Nina. In 1892, while the colonel was perfecting his invention, their youngest daughter Ethyl died at age four. The parents were utterly grief stricken. When Greenwood Cemetery was dedicated by the City of Shreveport in 1894, the Hancock tomb was among the very first monuments built there and was, in fact, the very first mausoleum in the cemetery. Ethyl, who had first been buried at Oakland Cemetery downtown, was moved there that year and thus became one of Greenwood's first interments.

Little Ethyl's embalmed body was laid to rest in a cast-iron coffin containing a glass faceplate, through which her face could be seen as though she were simply asleep. Mrs. Hancock placed a chair inside the vault of the tomb, and every evening she would visit the tomb and read bedtime stories to her daughter. The practice went on for years, and though the visits declined in frequency, they nevertheless remained regular. Nina Hancock's grief-driven eccentricity came to be well known in the city and prompted some speculation about her sanity.

Meanwhile, Milton, Nina and their surviving son and daughter moved from their then remote rural residence on Fairfield Avenue near Kings Highway to a more spacious home in the 1200 block of Texas Avenue (demolished in 1907, the site was long occupied by the Brenner's Furniture Company building, now the location of Ivan Smith Furniture). Hancock spent much of his time traveling. Mrs. Hancock stayed home with their children, both living and departed. Eventually, Nina snapped, wandering the streets at night and indulging what might be described as nymphomania. The reputation she earned as a result led to Colonel Hancock's separation from her and, eventually, to divorce. Later, Nina ended up living—at least for a time—the life of a prostitute.

In 1903, Colonel Hancock left Shreveport and moved to Los Angeles, California. Then forty-five years of age, he entered semiretirement after a decade of struggle and hard work building his company into the nation's top plow manufacturer. In Los Angeles, he remarried and lived comfortably with his new wife and his and Nina's surviving children. His well-earned relaxation was to be short-lived, however.

On July 29, 1905, Milton Taylor Hancock became an early casualty of the automobile age. Even in Los Angeles, cars were still rare in 1905. Horse-drawn vehicles had priority, and modern rules of the road were still largely nonexistent. On that fateful day, Colonel Hancock's sixteen-year-old son, Milton Jr., was at the wheel chauffeuring his father and stepmother, as he often did. According to a front-page story in the *Los Angeles Times*, a dairy wagon pulled into the path of the Hancocks' speeding car. Unable to avoid a collision, Milton Jr. struck the wagon, demolishing it and throwing his father out of the open automobile and into the street, where he was dragged some 125 feet to his death. It was an unfortunate and premature ending for a remarkable man.

Hancock's body was returned to Shreveport on July 23, 1906, just shy of a year after the accident that took his life. He was laid to rest beside his daughter Ethyl in the big tomb at Greenwood Cemetery. His other children, Milton Jr. and Edith, never returned to Shreveport.

The tales about the tomb, the chair for Nina Hancock and the bedtime stories for little Ethyl still remain in the shadowy legends of old Shreveport, even while Colonel Hancock, his marvelous plow and the fortune it made him have nearly been forgotten.

Andrew Querbes, Mayor and Business Leader

One of the outstanding figures in local history was Andrew Querbes, for many years the president of First National Bank, twice mayor of Shreveport and longtime area businessman. To this day, the name Querbes remains one of the city's most recognizable family names: there is Querbes Street

Andrew and Alexandrine Querbes (standing) with their grandchildren, mid-1930s. *Author's collection.*

in the Pierremont area; Querbes Park and Querbes Golf Course occupy the site of the old Broadmoor Country Club in the Broadmoor/South Highlands area; and Querbes and Nelson Insurance Company is one of the area's oldest and most respected businesses.

Not until 1881, however, did the name Querbes enter the roster of Shreveport's citizenry, and then only briefly. In that year, seventeen-year-old Andre, as he was then called (he is so listed in the city directory of that year), came to Shreveport to work as a clerk for a French grocer named C. Gouzy, whose store was in the 100 block of Commerce Street. By 1882, Andre had returned to the New Orleans area and did not move back to Shreveport until 1886. In that year, twenty-two-year-old Andrew (his name now anglicized) and his recently widowed mother came to Shreveport from Mandeville, and shortly thereafter he opened a grocery business, called the New Orleans Store, on Commerce Street. Eventually, he would own a great deal of property throughout downtown, including a substantial portion of the riverfront area.

Querbes's grocery business developed from a small retail store into a large wholesale firm. In 1902, he sold his business, concentrating on area politics. In 1896, he had been elected to the Caddo Parish Police Jury (now the Caddo Parish Commission), and 1902 saw his election as mayor of the city for a two-year term. Two years later, the voters returned him to office for a second mayoral term. During his tenure as Shreveport's chief executive, a new city hall was built at the northwest corner of Milam and Louisiana; it would continue to serve the city until 1958.

Querbes did not seek a third term as mayor in 1906, returning to business life as vice-president of First National Bank. Also that same year, he was instrumental in helping to organize the Louisiana State Fair, and a road at the fairgrounds honors his long commitment to that organization. In 1908, he became president of the First National Bank and in 1914 became president of the Louisiana Bankers Association. Also in 1914, Querbes was appointed to the board of Charity Hospital (now LSU Health Sciences Center) by Governor Ruffin G. Pleasant, a fellow Shreveporter.

Besides the State Fair, a board on which he remained from 1906 until his death thirty-three years later, he also helped organize the chamber of commerce in 1910 and was active in fundraising for the war effort during World War I, chairing the area's first and second Liberty Loan drives. He was also a longtime member of Holy Trinity Catholic Church.

Additionally, Andrew Querbes was involved in the ice and bottling business, associated with the Shreveport Ice and Brewing Company and president of the Shreveport Ice Delivery Company. It was his bottling firm that acquired Shreveport's first Coca-Cola franchise, a most lucrative investment, bringing bottled Coke to Shreveport not many years after it had first been successfully bottled at Vicksburg, Mississippi.

Querbes was president of the Louisiana Cotton Growers Cooperative Association and vice-president of the Shreveport Mutual Building Association, later to become First Federal Savings and Loan. He was also an active member of the Shreveport Rotary Club, in which he held several offices, and was active in the Shreveport Advertising Club, serving as its chairman in 1919 when the Ad Club published the first "view book" of Shreveport, a publication designed to promote the area to prospective businesses nationally.

Andrew Querbes was the son of Antoine Querbes and Louise Alterieu Querbes, who were from the vicinity of Marseille, France (the French pronunciation of the name is "kehrb"). While some members of the Querbes family migrated from southern France to Quebec (there is a Querbes Street in Montreal today), Andrew's parents came to the New Orleans area, where his father was a dry goods and grocery merchant both in New Orleans itself and in nearby Mandeville.

On February 12, 1889, Andrew Querbes married Alexandrine Ricou, daughter of prominent grocer Justin Ricou, for whom Ricou Street, in the Agurs area of Shreveport, is named. Thus the Querbes, Ricou and Gras families—for the local grocer and philanthropist Justin Gras was Justin Ricou's nephew—became connected.

The Querbeses had three children, Andrew Jr. and Randolph, who were both long associated with the Interstate Electric Company as well as with Shreveport Ice and Brewing, and Justin, who was the original Querbes of Querbes and Bourquin Insurance, which he co-founded in 1914 and later became Querbes and Nelson.

For many years, Andrew and Alexandrine Querbes resided in an ornate Victorian home at 417 Milam Street. Later they moved to 633 Jordan, where they were living when Andrew died in 1939. Alexandrine, who was five years his junior, survived him by eighteen years; both are buried at Forest Park Cemetery. Both the Milam Street house, with its intricate "gingerbread" detailing, and the stately Greek Revival home on Jordan Street are gone today. The Milam Street home, which became a boardinghouse after the Querbeses moved from it, was demolished in the early 1920s to build the Goldring's Building, itself torn down in 1996 along with the Ricou-Brewster Building next door (originally partly owned by Andrew Querbes, his wife and his brother-in-law), which had been built in 1924 on the site of the old Ricou house. The building that housed Andrew Querbes's New Orleans store still stands, however. Long home to the Kennedy Supply Company, the building is located at the southwest corner of Commerce and Milam Streets and now houses offices. Querbes and Nelson still occupies the 214 Milam Street building, built in 1871 as Tally's Opera House, that housed Querbes and Bourquin beginning in 1914.

W.K. Henderson, Radio Man

One of the great Shreveport biographies is that of iron magnate and radio broadcaster William Kennon Henderson Jr. Born in Bastrop in 1880 but raised in Jefferson, Texas, Henderson first rose to prominence in the early twentieth century as the owner of what was then the world's largest automobile garage. But he made his chief fortune in the timber and iron industries before becoming obsessed with the power and glory of the newfound radio broadcast industry and eventually falling victim to the Great Depression. The Federal Radio Commission (today the Federal Communications Commission) was formed in part to regulate the language and range of this broadcasting pioneer who dominated the airwaves of the 1920s as the nation's first "shock jock" and whose colorful storytelling and rambling political diatribes made his sign on catchphrase, "Hello world, doggone you!" known nationally.

W.K. Henderson was forty-two years old when he invested in his first radio station in 1923, a modest 250-watt operation to which he gave his initials: KWKH. Soon he discovered a disparity in how the government awarded frequencies and wattage, and he quickly grew weary of the favoritism shown northern stations. He began what would be a long and protracted battle for equality of the airwaves for Shreveport and the South in general. The twenties were a time of great prosperity for Henderson. He had recently taken over the reins of the Henderson Iron Works upon the death of his father and built the industry into the nation's sixth largest iron

W.K. Henderson. *Author's collection.*

company in a few short years. He and his wife, Josie Carter Henderson, and their two children wanted for nothing.

Henderson boasted that his multimillion-dollar business paid 10 percent of all city taxes, and through his position as vice-president and then president of the Shreveport Chamber of Commerce, he took an active role in the shaping of the burgeoning oil metropolis. At various times, he owned interests in the city's electric, gas, telephone and taxicab companies. His eccentricities included an affinity for the number thirteen and a penchant for "crisp" currency, which was created by meticulous ironing of his pocket money each morning. Henderson demanded loyalty but was also quick to reward it and demonstrated familial devotion to his friends.

In politics, W.K. promoted Al Smith for president in 1928 and was one of Huey Long's most influential backers. He gave Long unlimited free airtime on KWKH, which proved to be a decided advantage in his gubernatorial campaigns. But Will and Huey ultimately had a nasty falling out over Long's refusal to hold a special session of the legislature to pass a bill for Shreveport to acquire necessary land for the location of Barksdale Army Air Field. Long had no ill will toward Shreveport itself—indeed, it was his official city of residence—but he did have much toward Caddo Parish, which had been the only parish in the state not to support his free textbook plan. When Henderson devised a plan to locate the airfield in Bossier Parish yet still have it located in Shreveport by annexing the land into the city, Governor Long ultimately held the session and passed the bill, but not before being thoroughly reprimanded by Henderson on the air.

Known to many as "Old Man Henderson" because his radio voice sounded like that of an octogenarian even when he was in his forties, W.K. spoke on the radio whenever the mood suited him. With microphones on his office desk, his desk at home and even beside his bed, he preached his mind at all hours of the day and night. He rarely slept more than four or five hours a night, and his employees were expected to be permanently "on call."

Upset with his station's frequency allocation and wattage, Henderson would often change his assigned dial position at will and increase power as much as tenfold. At night, he would focus his signal into what he termed "a wide highway through middle America" and invite those who didn't want to listen to "stay the hell off!" Complaints flooded the FRC about the powerful and profane broadcasts originating from Shreveport and beaming northward into Canada. Farmers couldn't get their local stations' weather reports and Bible thumpers questioned Henderson's free usage of "hell," "damn" and often much worse. W.K. challenged the Commerce Department on this point, saying that it had no authority to govern the airwaves (based on the Radio Act of 1912), and defending his language as "nothing that can't be found in the Bible." He ultimately won his way but agreed to tone down his language in exchange for an increase in wattage and a better dial position.

Henderson's favorite topics for his nightly discourse were Prohibition ("It sure is hot tonight and [rattling his glass] this ain't iced tea I'm drinking!"), the FRC itself ("They give the northern stations all the power they want but expect *us* to go in the basement and whisper") and his opposition to chain stores ("As a boy, I peeked out from behind the barn once and saw Papa unload a stallion who proceeded to give our mare the same treatment you folks are getting from the chain stores"). He regularly challenged his detractors to "kiss my ass" and then added, for the FRC's benefit, that "it's tied up out back and waitin' for ya."

But it was the anti–chain store movement that became the obsession of Will Henderson and drove his nightly tirades against the Piggly Wiggly chain—"that Sears Rareback outfit." At the dawn of the Great Depression, he formed a national organization called the Merchants' Minute Men, a coalition of small businessmen who routinely went into chain stores seeking out infractions such as selling a five-pound bag of sugar that weighed only four and a half pounds. Henderson took personal delight in reading the offending chain store owner's name and phone number over the air, and soon children everywhere would warn their parents, "Don't go into chain stores; old Man Henderson is watching you!"

Will Henderson shared the growing national belief that chains came into a community and took away business from local mom and pop operations and rerouted taxable revenue away from the community (a fear still played upon by opponents of large discount firms today). He believed that if these industry giants were to grow unchecked, it would spell the end of small business in America.

Privately, Henderson was a generous man, purchasing automobiles for friends, putting employees through college and even law school and wiring the homes of people who lacked them with electrical connections and telephones. He was vocally anti-union but provided housing, full insurance and medical benefits and the best possible working conditions, including twice-daily coffee breaks for all his employees—this long before it was required or even customary to do so. He also made a practice of hiring the homeless and disenfranchised and was known for treating each with respect.

Henderson's radio station, KWKH, was located at Kennonwood, his estate just north of Shreveport, which became a commune of sorts during the Depression, serving as the residence of all radio personnel as well as many "guests" who took their host up on his generous radio invitation to "come visit us and stay as long as you like." In response to government pressure to feature more live programming instead of recordings, one summer Henderson offered up Simeon Oliver, an Eskimo pianist, and Chief Kiutus Tecumseh, a Washington state apple grower and traveling tenor who lectured on Indian rights. Visitors would be given a case of apples by the chief and be allowed to tour the grounds, including the transmission room, where, according to W.K.'s son Carter, "flames leapt from the super-charged equipment" and frightened the guests.

Henderson made lasting enemies of Clarence Saunders, who blamed him for having to sell Piggly Wiggly; Senator Clarence Dill, who led the government inquiries into KWKH practices; and oilman William Skelly, owner of Tulsa radio station KVOO, who tried unsuccessfully to acquire KWKH's frequency. Incidentally, Skelly's daughter Carolyn and her husband, Freeman Burford of the Crystal Oil Company, were Shreveport residents at the time.

But Henderson's fortunes suffered greatly during the Depression years, and despite a radio team that worked the final two years for room and board only, the station had to be sold in 1933 in a vain attempt to hang on to the family ironworks.

Looking back on the Henderson era, one can see the incredible influence of this man and his legacy. He and his engineers were the first to broadcast records directly from the needle, bypassing the standard method of placing a microphone in front of a conical speaker. They, too, were the first to use two interlinked turntables to fade from one record into the next.

Shortly after selling his beloved station to a consortium of local investors who promised to retain the integrity of KWKH and offer regular forums to the displaced owner, Will was betrayed by these same colleagues, who were quick to affiliate with the CBS chain radio network. An advertisement in the Shreveport newspapers several years later announced that Old Man Henderson was still around, only now without money, and would welcome any honest business propositions because "with me, two and two still make four." He made occasional radio speeches against the Commercial National Bank, which had reorganized to the detriment of its investors and the enrichment of its trustees, but by and large Henderson's crusading days were over by 1933.

William Kennon Henderson Jr. died in 1945 from complications of a wasp sting. Nearly broke and virtually helpless after suffering a series of strokes, he stated shortly before his death, "I was right, you know...about the chain stores...I can't even feed or bathe myself now but I still have my radio."

The Radio Act of 1927 that created the FRC/FCC was written in large measure to regulate one man, W.K. Henderson, and those like him who might follow. Yet it contains many passages detailing the assignment of frequencies and wattage that still are law today, passages fought for long and hard by W.K. Henderson and gained at terrific personal cost.

KWKH itself went on to become one of the nation's flagship stations, creating the legendary Louisiana Hayride program in 1948. It eventually grew into the fifty-thousand-watt giant of Henderson's dreams, but at the end of the twentieth century it was acquired by the biggest chain radio concern in the world: Clear Channel. No doubt "Old Man Henderson" is spinning in his grave at Greenwood Cemetery.

William Edenborn: Baron of Business

One of the most prominent businessmen in the history of this region was a native of Germany named William Edenborn. When he died in Shreveport on May 14, 1926, at the age of seventy-eight years he was one of the wealthiest men in the nation. Obituaries for him ran in such dailies as the *Wall Street Journal* and the *New York Times*, as well as in Shreveport and New Orleans papers and, indeed, newspapers the nation over.

William Edenborn's name is not as widely known today, and he sleeps in relative obscurity beneath a large but simple monument at Forest Park Cemetery on Shreveport's St. Vincent Avenue. Yet this was a man who built several great businesses, helped to fence the ranches of the West and created a railroad.

Wilhelm Edenborn was born in Westphalia, Prussia (in what is now the German state of Lower Saxony), on March 20, 1848. In 1867, at the age of nineteen, he immigrated to the United States, anglicizing his first name to William. In Germany, Edenborn had worked as an apprentice in blacksmith shops and had learned to make nails of all sorts; in the United

William Edenborn. *Author's collection.*

States, this became his specialty. After a stay in New York, he moved to Pittsburgh, Pennsylvania, and then to Cincinnati, Ohio. In 1870, he settled in St. Louis, there inventing a machine for making barbed wire, the nucleus of his future wealth.

Edenborn organized the first wire mill in St. Louis, followed by other mills elsewhere. The westward expansion of the nation created a great demand for barbed wire as well as for simple wire for fencing. Edenborn's firm also made wire for telegraph and telephone communications, new and cutting-edge technology in the last quarter of the nineteenth century. In 1899, he incorporated the American Steel and Wire Company. Two years later, he sold it for $100 million (about twenty-five times that in today's dollars) to J.P. Morgan who merged it with Carnegie Steel Company, also acquired in 1901, to form the United States Steel Corporation.

In the early 1890s, Edenborn, who had frequently visited the Deep South and the Southwest in conjunction with his wire business, decided to build a railroad from New Orleans to Shreveport in order to link the Gulf of Mexico to east Texas by rail. Construction of the Louisiana Railway & Navigation Company (the LR&N) began in earnest in 1897. The line was built in stages over the next decade, finally reaching New Orleans in 1907, thus creating the shortest, fastest rail route from north Louisiana to south Louisiana yet built at the time. By 1922, the LR&N extended to McKinney, Texas, northeast of Dallas.

While building the LR&N, Edenborn moved to Louisiana, establishing residences at both Shreveport and New Orleans. Over $20 million of his personal wealth was invested in the LR&N, and it is estimated that by 1926 he had put another $50 million into Louisiana's economy via payrolls, taxes and other costs of the business. No money other than his own went into the LR&N, and Edenborn oversaw personally every aspect of the railroad's management.

For many years, William Edenborn sat on the board of directors of the U.S. Steel Corporation, and he was long listed among the nation's wealthiest men. He was a benefactor of numerous charitable and philanthropic causes, though the full extent of his generosity is unknown since many of his gifts were given anonymously. Despite his place among the great capitalists of the Gilded Age, Edenborn remained a staunch Democrat all his life.

It is said that he could have made many millions more had he followed the cutthroat business tactics that made many other multimillionaires of that day and age, yet he died with a reputation of fairness in his business dealings and in his relationships with his many employees. He kept a low profile in every aspect of his life, shunned ostentation and avoided society gatherings. Whenever asked for a public statement regarding any aspect of his personal or business life, he would reply with courtesy, "I have nothing to say at this time, thank you."

Among his other endeavors, Edenborn was a cotton planter, a grower of silkworms and producer of silk (though his attempts to introduce the silk business to Louisiana failed) and a lumberman. He was also an investor in many varied business concerns, especially agricultural ones. In 1918, Edenborn was arrested and briefly detained by federal authorities in Louisiana for allegedly making pro-German comments when he voiced his opinion that the United States should not fear a German sea attack but rather had more to be concerned about its alliance with Great Britain once the war ended.

On October 5, 1886, William Edenborn married Sarah Drain, then thirty, of St. Louis. The couple maintained a home there until 1898, when they moved to the Shreveport area. In 1906, 8018 Hampson Street in the Uptown area of New Orleans became their home, though their principal place of residence was at Emden, their large plantation in Winn Parish, southeast Shreveport, named for his birthplace in Germany. There, on May 7, 1926, William Edenborn was stricken with apoplexy and rushed to Shreveport aboard his private train car.

Taken to Schumpert Hospital, he lingered for a week without fully regaining consciousness. When he died at 1:32 a.m. on May 14, his wife of forty-nine years was at his side, as were Dr. James E. Knighton and Dr. Rawley M. Penick, chief surgeon of the LR&N. Edenborn's personal wealth at the time of his death was estimated at $100 million (more than $2 billion in today's terms). He was laid to rest in section N of Forest Park Cemetery on St. Vincent Avenue. Twelve truckloads of flowers and a funeral procession fifteen blocks long accompanied his remains to the cemetery. His widow became president of the LR&N on May 19, 1926, the first woman in American history to head a major railroad. She survived her husband by eighteen years, coming to rest beside him in 1944. Although they were the parents of two daughters, both children predeceased the Edenborns and no direct heirs to the vast fortune were left behind at their deaths. An important street in the New Orleans suburb of Metairie is named for William Edenborn, though no memorial exists to him in Shreveport, other than his tombstone and his legacy.

H.L. Hunt and Shreveport

Once upon a time, one of the world's richest men, if not *the* richest, lived in Shreveport. His name was H.L. Hunt, and his story is the stuff of legends.

Haroldson Lafayette Hunt Jr. was born in Carson Township, Illinois, in 1889. In 1905, Hunt left home and traveled west, working at various odd jobs and gambling. After his father died in 1911, Hunt went home to collect his modest inheritance and then moved to Lake Village, Arkansas. Initially a cotton farmer, Hunt soon got into land speculation and then

H.L. Hunt. *Author's collection.*

more gambling. There he also met and married his first wife, Lyda Bunker, in 1914.

Soon after the discovery of the Smackover oil field in El Dorado, Arkansas, H.L. started drilling for oil. His first well was successful and he soon moved to El Dorado. In 1925, as the boom in El Dorado was winding down, Hunt sold his operation and traveled to Florida, becoming a real estate speculator.

In Florida that same year, he met his second wife, Frania Tye (originally Tiburski). The problem was, he was not divorced from Lyda. Using the name "Franklin" Hunt, however, H.L. and Frania married nevertheless, honeymooning in New Orleans and then setting up residence in Shreveport, where they lived for a time at 330 Herndon and for a time at 514 Gladstone, in both cases in extremely unpretentious houses.

Hunt managed his two bigamous marriages, both of which resulted in families—six children with Lyda and four with Frania—by traveling at least twice weekly between El Dorado and Shreveport, maintaining offices in both cities. In Shreveport, Hunt's office was located in the Washington-Youree Hotel. Hunt was also a member of the First Baptist Church of Shreveport.

During this time, an investment that Hunt had made in east Texas real estate paid off in a big way, with H.L. became a leading independent producer in the largest oil field discovered up to that time, the great east Texas oil field near Kilgore. To give an idea of the size and importance of this field, it should be noted that crude oil was priced at just over one dollar per barrel when the field was discovered and, owing to the oversupply the massive field created, fell to fifteen cents per barrel once production began. Throughout the Great Depression, this area of the country never suffered an economic hardship.

Despite the wealth of his wells, however, Hunt had invested heavily in the east Texas field and was initially short on ready cash with which to drill further. He tried to borrow money from the two largest Shreveport banks to develop his east Texas leases but they foolishly refused to loan money on in-ground reserves. Consequently, Hunt went to the First National Bank in Dallas and obtained the loans he needed. This was the beginning of the end of Shreveport's primacy as the center of the nation's oil and gas industry.

Hunt moved his first family by Lyda from El Dorado to Tyler, Texas, and then ultimately to Dallas in 1937. It was in the early 1940s that his bigamous marriage to Frania was revealed. The couple broke up in 1942, and H.L. set up trusts for his children by Frania and agreed to provide for her as well. Only after Hunt's third wife Ruth died in 1975 did Frania sue H.L.'s estate for half of its assets. Her case, heard in federal court in Shreveport in 1978, resulted in a $9.2 million settlement in her favor.

Although enormously wealthy in the oil business, Hunt also dabbled in other businesses, most notably food and cosmetics. Although hugely successful in his oil ventures, he was less so in his others. He had fun with them, though, even exhibiting annually at the Louisiana State Fair in Shreveport, where he manned his own food products booth. For a time in the early 1970s, his promotion of the benefits of aloe vera was successful, though the widespread use of aloe proved to be little more than a flash in the pan.

Lyda died in 1955, and two years later Hunt married his secretary and longtime mistress, Ruth Ray, by whom he already had four children ranging in age from seven to fourteen at the time. Although Ruth tried to bring together Hunt's fourteen children, there were undeniable and understandable tensions between the children of H.L.'s three separate families.

From Hunt's marriage to Lyda, his sons Nelson Bunker and William Herbert were later notorious for their attempt to corner the U.S. silver market in the late 1970s. Ultimately, their machinations drove the price of silver to an all-time high of fifty dollars per ounce in January 1980. The silver investments were, to say the least, bizarre and involved the brothers buying up millions of pounds of silver (much of it stored on their Circle K Ranch in Texas and later, at great expense, in Switzerland) and using it to leverage various financial deals with such entities as the Shah of Iran and the Marcoses of the Philippines. It also led to calamity when financial setbacks related to the oil industry forced the brothers to liquidate their silver holdings shortly after the metal's price had peaked. The plummet of silver from fifty to seventeen dollars per ounce, virtually overnight, caused the Treasury Department and the Federal Reserve Bank to set up round-the-clock silver monitoring lest the federal government need to step in to prevent a financial panic.

Ultimately, the silver debacle led to Bunker's filing for bankruptcy in 1988. When his older sister, philanthropist Margaret Hunt Hill, asked him what he had been trying to accomplish, Bunker replied that he was "just trying to make a little money."

It was just before the silver buy-up by his sons began that H.L. Hunt died, his death occurring on November 29, 1974, in Dallas (his home there, near White Rock Park, was a replica—at least on the exterior—of George Washington's Mount Vernon, and also bore that name). H.L.

Hunt is buried at Sparkman-Hillcrest Cemetery on Northwest Highway in Dallas.

Hunt's other children include petroleum executives H.L. "Hassie" Hunt III and Ray Lee Hunt, Rosewood Hotels CEO Caroline Rose Hunt, U.S. Ambassador to Austria Swanee Hunt, author Helen LeKelly Hunt, Kansas City Chiefs football team owner (and founder of the American Football League, of which the short-lived Shreveport Steamer team was a part) Lamar Hunt, radio personality June Hunt, Constructivist Foundation founder Hugh Hunt, Haroldina Franch Hunt, Helen Hunt Kreiling (yes, H.L. had two daughters named Helen) and Howard Lee Hunt. The last four named were by Frania Tye and, with the exception of Hugh, who was born in Dallas, were born and raised in Shreveport.

Frania Tye married a Hunt Company employee, Colonel John W. Lee, in 1942, just two weeks after her separation from H.L.; she died in Atlanta in 2001 at the age of ninety-seven.

CULTURAL LEADERS

Professor W.C. O'Hare, Composer

In his time, composer William Christopher O'Hare of Shreveport was one of America's musical celebrities. A native of Washington, D.C., O'Hare came to Shreveport in 1887 at the age of twenty to be the first musical director of the Grand Opera House, which opened that year. He quickly became part of the community, and his talents were much in demand. A Catholic, he became choir director of Holy Trinity Church but over the next decade would also serve St. Mark's Episcopal, First Baptist and First Methodist Churches as well as B'nai Zion Temple in this same capacity. He married a local girl, Mary Carlotta "Lottie" Slater, a native of nearby Marshall, Texas, in 1890.

O'Hare was a classically trained musician, and by 1896, he had taken the post of professor of music at the Kate Nelson Seminary, a prestigious Victorian-era day and boarding school for young ladies once located at the northeast corner of Texas and Grand Avenues (Grand Avenue is today Elvis Presley Avenue). In fact, he and his wife Lottie lived at 134 Grand, close by the school and just a few doors off Texas Avenue, then more a major thoroughfare than now.

Although O'Hare was white, much of "the Avenue," as Texas Avenue was known—especially the blocks between nearby Christian Street (now Austin Place) and Hope Street—was the center of black life in Shreveport during that era. Along this strip performed many itinerant black musicians who were ultimately to go on to become major figures in the jazz, blues and ragtime genres of American music. Many of these figures also played

W.C. O'Hare (right) with wife Lottie. *Courtesy of Sue O'Hare Atalla.*

in the bawdy houses of the nearby red-light district, as they did in New Orleans, Dallas and other cities and towns of the region.

It is not certain just how O'Hare became acquainted with many of the black musicians of the Avenue, for though close to his residence it was many miles away from him socially and culturally. But it is certain that he did become acquainted with them. Indeed, he seems to have played a major role in legitimizing and popularizing the ragtime and blues music that he heard, something few in his position were willing to do. Ultimately, O'Hare was to become an important link between black and white musical cultures.

That O'Hare knew Scott Joplin, a Texarkana native and major figure in the history of ragtime music, is definite, and it is believed that O'Hare lent Joplin assistance in establishing a name for himself. Likewise, O'Hare was well acquainted with composer and jazz pianist Ferdinand LeMenthe of New Orleans, better known as Jelly Roll Morton, who wrote a famous ragtime composition called "The Shreveport Stomp." O'Hare and Joplin were about the same age, though O'Hare was somewhat older than Morton. By the time of his association with Morton, O'Hare had left Louisiana and was well ensconced in the music world of New York. As an employee of the Witmark Music Company of New York, O'Hare would assist other struggling jazz artists from the South make a name for themselves on the national scene as well. While he was helping to launch their careers, he was also busy working on his own.

Although O'Hare is best remembered for his ragtime compositions, most of his own music was not jazz or ragtime at all. Among his works were a "mystery dance" called "Heliobas" and two theatrical-musical "spectacular" productions called *The Evil Eye* and *Hermann the Great*. He wrote for piano, orchestra, band and voice, and was noted for his sacred as well as his secular music. His rendition of "Te Deum" was first performed in St. Mark's Episcopal Church, then located at the northwest corner of Fannin and Market Streets, and his "We Bend" premiered at the B'nai Zion Temple, then located one door west of St. Mark's on Fannin. "We Bend" was a popular piece for Jewish High Holy Days services at the turn of the twentieth century. Shreveport's Grand Opera House (which stood where the Chase Bank Tower stands today) saw the first performances of most of O'Hare's major secular works, several of which went on to success in New York.

O'Hare's waltz "The Awakening of Venus" was much admired by no less a figure than John Philip Sousa, who did for O'Hare what O'Hare later did for others. In September 1898, Sousa introduced one of O'Hare's jazz-inspired pieces called "Levee Revels: An Afro-American Cane-Hop" at the St. Louis Exposition. "Levee Revels" was a cakewalk piece, a musical type inspired by plantation dances and melodies that could often be heard on Shreveport's Texas Avenue. Another such piece was "Cotton Pickers," which was a hit in New York at the beginning of the 1900s. Interesting to note is the coincidental fact that modern-day Shreveport's annual autumn arts festival is called the Red River Revel and is held on the riverfront, which in O'Hare's day was commonly known as the levee.

Other significant O'Hare works include "The C.S.A. Grand Medley" (1892), "The Cotton Pickers" (1894), "Plantation Pastimes" (1895), "The

Awakening of Venus" (a waltz), "Southern Interlude" and many popular songs such as "Where the River Shannon Flows," "Too-Ra Loo-Ra Loo-Ra," "The Witch Behind the Moon" (composed for *The Wizard of Oz*) and numerous show tunes, including pieces commissioned and/or used by Florenz Ziegfeld, Manuel Klein and Karl Hoschna. Many of these came after O'Hare left Shreveport for New York.

In 1899, O'Hare resided at 702 Crockett Street but in 1900 he changed his place of residence to the then fashionable City Hotel at 221 Milam, where he arranged the entertainment schedule. By 1901, however, he was frequently traveling between Shreveport, New Orleans and New York as his musical career advanced. Finally, he moved to New York altogether, taking a position with the M. Witmark and Sons Music Company, a major sheet music publisher and, much later, a recording company and residing on Lexington Avenue. Lottie and the O'Hare children did not make the move initially, and when they did, New York ultimately broke the family up. Within a short time of the move, the O'Hares separated and within the decade had divorced, a rare occurrence in that era for a Catholic couple.

In New York, O'Hare's work with Witmark focused on the publication of popular music, especially that of the ragtime genre. An important collaboration was with the composer Victor Herbert, with whom O'Hare co-composed and for whom he arranged a significant body of musical compositions. Herbert was in his day one of America's—and the world's—most popular composers, and his regular appearances at the Shreveport Grand Opera House no doubt owed much to O'Hare's influence there, which continued well after his departure from the opera house and from Shreveport. Among the O'Hare-Herbert collaborations were "If I Were on the Stage" (from *Mlle. Modiste*, 1905), "Selection" (*Old Dutch*, 1909) and "The Naughty Marietta Waltzes" (*Naughty Marietta*, 1911). O'Hare's "Sand Dancers," of the same period, is clearly inspired by Herbert's style.

William Christopher O'Hare never returned to Shreveport, at least not as a resident. He remained in New York for nearly half a century, composing for movie houses and later for movies and composing, arranging and directing music for churches. He worked as a church organist and choir director until his death in 1943, and he taught music as well. Though much of his most notable work occurred after his departure from Shreveport, William Christopher O'Hare nevertheless played a vital role in the area's musical history, and in that of the nation, in the early twentieth century.

William Kinney, Sculptor and Stonemason

In Shreveport's older cemeteries, there is found a variety of strikingly beautiful and artistically fine stone carvings. Some of these monuments, particularly those at Oakland Cemetery downtown, Shreveport's oldest public cemetery, have suffered from deterioration over the decades. Others are as pristine as the day they were set in place.

Of the creators of these works of art, the most significant by far was a stonecutter named William B. Kinney. Born in Ireland in 1830, Kinney came to America about 1850, settling in Shreveport and establishing himself not only as a maker of tombstones but also as a stonemason and sculptor early on. He set up his stonecutting business here in or before 1853 (the date of his earliest known signed stone) and continued in operation, either as an independent marble cutter or in partnership, until 1899.

Kinney's operation was located on Jewell Street, between Lawrence and Hope Streets, during the 1850s, just two blocks west of Oakland Cemetery. Soon he became the city's premier stonemason, receiving the lion's share of monument orders, most of which previously had been given to out-of-

WM. KINNEY,

Manufacturer and Dealer in

Foreign and Domestic Marble, Monuments, Head Stones, Tablets, Etc., of Latest Design,

TERRA COTTA VASES, FOR CEMETERY AND GARDEN ADORNMENT.

Designs Furnished on Application.

Travis Street, next door to the Baptist Church.

SHREVEPORT, LA.

Advertisement for Kinney Marble Works from the *Shreveport Commercial Directory for 1875. Author's collection.*

town firms, as Shreveport had no permanent professional stonecutters in operation prior to Kinney's arrival. Although a few itinerant stonemasons are known to have passed through the city or come in from elsewhere for brief stays while working on particular projects, none remained permanently until Kinney.

At the outbreak of the Civil War, the thirty-one-year-old Kinney left his successful business to join the Confederate army, becoming captain of Company F of the Third Louisiana Infantry.

After the war's end, Kinney returned to Shreveport but had to reestablish his business from the ground up. He entered into a short-lived partnership with a marble cutter named Warren Hecox under the name Hecox & Kinney. Hecox had previously been in business on his own, though only one stone signed by him alone is known. It is the monument of his brother, Thomas W. Hecox, who was killed in the Civil War, and it bears the mark "Hecox & Co., Shreveport, LA."

Many monuments bearing the signature "Hecox & Kinney" or merely "H. & K." can be found throughout the area's older cemeteries, especially Oakland. The partnership was short-lived, however, as Hecox died in 1870. Thus, by 1871, William Kinney was again a sole proprietor, and stones signed by him at this time bear only the signature "*Kinney*" or "*W. Kinney*." Kinney's signature marks are usually found in the lower right-hand corner of the stone close to the base, or on the base of the stone itself. Only occasionally do his marks appear elsewhere and only occasionally are they not carved in italics. In the 1875 City Directory, he appears as an independent marble cutter located on Travis Street, one door in from the southeast corner with Market Street. Advertising directs customers to his marble works on "Travis Street, next the Baptist Church," today the middle of the south side of the 200 block of Travis.

During the late 1870s, Kinney was again in partnership, this time with a Mr. Garrett (probably J.W. Garrett). This partnership, like that with Hecox, appears to have been short-lived. Garrett seems not to have been a stonecutter himself but rather a general merchandise dealer. It is possible that Kinney's monuments were sold through Garrett's business and that Garrett provided capital for Kinney's business. Stones cut during this period bear the marks "*K & G*" or "*Kinney & Garrett*."

During the early 1880s, Kinney formed a partnership with stonemason John W. Taber, and for a time there was a third partner as well, Michael

Dwyer. By 1884, however, all three partners had gone their separate ways. Kinney and Taber were both working independently by the mid-1880s and Dwyer appears to have left Shreveport before 1884.

Throughout the remainder of his career, William Kinney's marble works was located in the 500 block of Texas Street, opposite the Caddo Parish Courthouse. All stones carved by Kinney after 1881 bear only the name "*Kinney*" in italics. Some later stones attributed to Kinney's workshop bear no mark at all but owe their attributions to distinctive similarities with other known Kinney works.

During his long career, William Kinney was north Louisiana's most prolific and artistic monument maker. His designs vary widely; several are original and quite distinctive. His signed stones can be found in Shreveport's Oakland, Greenwood, Hebrew Rest, Summer Grove and St. Joseph Cemeteries. Works by Kinney can also be found in rural cemeteries around Shreveport, northwest Louisiana and east Texas, including Scottsville, Marshall and Karnack.

Although a Roman Catholic, William Kinney was adept at Hebrew carving. His work in Hebrew lettering is intricate and finely wrought, showing a familiarity with the language and the Jewish faith far beyond simple stencil carving. His Hebrew takes many stylistic forms, and it would appear that, at least by later life, he had acquired a fair command of the intricacies of the language. In 1869, he was hired to execute all of the marble work on the new B'nai Zion Synagogue on Fannin Street. He also did marble work for local churches and public buildings, some of which (particularly cornerstones) survives and is also often signed. His primary vocation, however, was in the making of funerary monuments, at which craft he excelled.

William B. Kinney died in 1907 and is buried at Oakland Cemetery next to his wife, Clara Geisse Kinney, long the bookkeeper for the Kinney Marble Works, and two of their children and one grandchild. Clara died in 1918. Curiously, Kinney's own monument is a simple and impersonal commercial stone with only a stylized Confederate battle flag setting it apart from other mundane markers of similar design. It stands almost inconspicuously among the elaborate works of art wrought by the talented man whose remains lie beneath.

JOSEPH DAMBLY, PHOTOGRAPHER, ENGRAVER AND FORENSICS PIONEER

A century ago, Shreveport's premier photographer was Joseph Dambly of Dambly Studios, long a landmark of Milam Street's 500 block, opposite the courthouse. While the best-known images of Shreveport's growth and development are by Burch and William Grabill, the father and son proprietors of Grabill Studios, they were not the first. Mose Kaufmann, Charles Robertshaw and T.M. Elliot produced many of the earliest known views of Shreveport buildings and streetscapes that can be positively attributed to a particular photographer, but the most prolific before the Grabills came onto the scene in 1919 was Joseph Dambly.

Beginning in 1899, the year he moved to Shreveport from Monroe, Joseph Dambly embarked upon a one-man crusade to chronicle the city in pictures. His large sepia images of Shreveport, mounted on cardboard backing and signed "Dambly," were prominently displayed in the Louisiana Purchase Exposition of 1904, held in St. Louis. Today, these images are in the collections of the Louisiana State Museum in New Orleans. Other views of Shreveport, made on behalf of the city's Progressive League, forerunner to the chamber of commerce, appear in early photo publications such as the Foster and Glassell Company's promotional booklet *Souvenir of Shreveport* (1902), the Progressive League's *Shreveport of Today* (1904) and the *Shreveport Journal*'s photo book *Shreveport: Queen City of the Southwest* (1905). His images also appear in magazines such as the short-lived *Pierian*, first published in 1903, and the New Orleans–based *Men and Matters* magazine, which covered topics of Louisiana interest in the 1890s and early 1900s.

Joseph Dambly in his studio, circa 1900. *Courtesy of LSUS Noel Memorial Library Archives.*

Joseph Dambly was born in St. Cloud, Minnesota, on June 30, 1867, the seventh of ten children of Jacob and Katherine Herges Dambly, natives of Koblenz, Germany, who came to the United States in 1857. Joseph went to school in St. Cloud and studied at the Minnesota State Teachers College before going to work in the general merchandise business. An older brother, William, was a photographer, and Joseph became interested in photography as well. In 1889, the two young men decided to take a trip across the country and photograph America. Their tour took them from their native Minnesota, through Wisconsin and Iowa and then south through Missouri, Tennessee, Mississippi and Louisiana.

It was in Louisiana that the brothers decided to end their journey. They never returned to St. Cloud but instead opened a studio in Baton Rouge in 1890. But Joseph never cared for Baton Rouge, and he decided to return to a town they had stopped in earlier on their cross-country trip, Monroe. In 1894, he sold his share of the studio to William and opened a studio in Monroe, then the only photographic studio in that town. In Monroe, he met a young lady named Alice Dudley when she sat for her photograph. The two were married on December 19, 1895.

In 1899, the Damblys moved to Shreveport, a city with several studios already in operation but a much larger community with greater prospects for growth. Although initially a portrait studio, the Dambly Studio soon expanded its business to include commercial work as Joseph Dambly's personal love of photographing buildings and city scenes became known. First located at 518 McNeill Street, Dambly relocated to 513 Milam a few years later. By 1903, Dambly, while still located on McNeill Street, was also shooting photographs for the city's newspapers. Indeed, his newspaper work was ultimately to change the direction of his life and career.

Prior to the middle part of the first decade of the twentieth century Shreveport's newspaper publishers—a market dominated by the *Shreveport Times*, the *Journal* and the *Caucasian*—had no local photoengraving firm to translate news photographs into printable form. In our age of computers, this seems difficult to comprehend, but a century ago it was a major production to include photographs in the newspaper. Only very large cities with the capacity for fast photoengraving could run news photos in the paper on a regular basis, if at all. Locally, the papers had to depend upon engraved sketches and other nonphotographic illustrations to accompany news stories. When special "souvenir editions" or "photogravure" pullout sections were published, such papers were huge productions, relying on out-of-town engravers to make the photographs printable.

Joseph Dambly changed that. In 1904, in addition to his photographic business, he established the first photoengraving plant in Shreveport, indeed the first to be located between St. Louis and New Orleans and between Dallas and Memphis. Newspapers, advertising agencies and printing companies from towns and cities within this huge area came to rely on Dambly's ability to provide photographic printing plates quickly (within hours) and efficiently. That efficiency and reliability led to the company's eventual name, Reliance Engraving. In 1920, he sold his photographic business to Burch Grabill and in 1921 sold Reliance Engraving to Porter E. Dozier, who changed the firm's name to Shreveport Engraving Company.

Although Dambly continued to work for Shreveport Engraving in an advisory capacity, he now turned the focus of his interests from photography and engraving to the fledgling science of fingerprint identification, which had fascinated him since he had done photographic work on a contract basis for the Shreveport Police Department a few years earlier. For a time during the twenties, Dambly worked in the fingerprint bureau of the SPD, but in 1928, with the creation of the Louisiana State Bureau of Identification (LBI), he went to work in its Shreveport office, specializing in fingerprint and photo identification work.

Considered a leader in the science of fingerprint and photographic identification, Joseph Dambly was offered an appointment with the State Bureau of Identification's main office in Baton Rouge by Governor Huey P. Long. In 1930, Dambly and his family moved there—the city he had left thirty-six years earlier and in which his brother William still resided—where he continued to serve as LBI investigator under the governorships of Long, Alvin O. King, O.K. Allen and James A. Noe. In 1936, he returned to Shreveport, going back to work for Shreveport Engraving, which in 1933 had been acquired jointly by the *Shreveport Times* and *Shreveport Journal*. After 1954, the company was a component of Newspaper Production Company, the result of the joint operating agreement—one of the first in American newspaper history—between the two papers. Dambly retired from the company in 1948; his son, William—named for Dambly's brother—also worked for Shreveport Engraving for many years as an engineer, retiring in the 1970s.

In addition to his accomplishments as a photographer, engraver and fingerprint expert, Joseph Dambly also served on the Shreveport City Council from 1906 to 1910 and was a member of Rettig's Band, a local brass band from the 1890s to the 1910s that included a number of prominent Shreveport names in its company. He and his wife were also among the first members of St. John Berchmans Catholic Church, established in 1902; today it is the Cathedral of the Diocese of Shreveport.

Although the Damblys resided for a time above the photo studio, their first house in Shreveport was a spacious one-story Victorian home at 1535 Irving Place (1425 Irving prior to street renumbering in 1906). The family later lived at 425 Dalzell and then at 230 Rutherford. All three homes still stand, though the Rutherford Street house has since been divided into apartments.

After his wife's death in August 1956 at the age of eighty-four, Joseph Dambly sold the place on Rutherford and moved in with his daughter, Kathryn, at 1021 Princeton Street in Bossier City. He died on March 17, 1958, three months shy of his ninety-first birthday. Many years before, in 1903, when their infant son Victor died at the age of four months, the Damblys had purchased a lot at Greenwood Cemetery. When Alice died, however, she was buried at Forest Park and Victor was moved there to rest near his mother. Alice's mother, Katherine Dudley, who later in life had lived with her daughter's family in Shreveport, and who was buried in the Greenwood lot in 1913, was also moved to Forest Park. Although the lot at Greenwood was sold to a family named Watkins—who since have used it three times for family burials—the name "Dambly" is still prominent on the lot's concrete steps. Kathryn Dambly, the daughter with whom Joseph lived during his final years, died in 1972; her brother William died in 1981.

Joseph Dambly was a pioneer in many fields. He was a pioneer photographer and the creator of the first important photographic chronicle of Shreveport's growth, a pioneer in making it possible for newspapers to publish photographs of breaking news and a pioneer in the science of fingerprint identification. Though now we hardly give such things a thought, in Dambly's era they were cutting-edge technology. How wonderful that Joe Dambly lived to see the technologies he pioneered evolve into commonplace practice that was taken virtually for granted. The name Joseph Dambly may not be widely remembered today, but his accomplishments are not forgotten.

MARY MILES MINTER, SIREN OF THE SILENT SCREEN

In her day, she was the most famous celebrity Shreveport had produced, and although her name is little noted now outside of the circles of early film enthusiasts and scholars of American film history, she remains one of the most important Shreveporters of the entertainment world. She was Mary Miles Minter, a silent film actress whose name, in the 1910s, was universally recognized.

Mary Miles Minter was the stage name of Juliet Reilly, born in Shreveport on April 1, 1902 (some sources give her birth date as April 25, 1902). She made her debut on the New York stage at the age of six and soon thereafter rose, largely through her mother's ceaseless prodding and machinations, to become one of the best-known stars in the nascent film industry of the early twentieth century, though her career was to be shattered by one of the century's most notorious Hollywood scandals in

Mary Miles Minter. *Author's collection.*

1922. A year later, at twenty-one years of age, she altogether vanished from the screen.

But although once extremely famous, Mary Miles Minter is nevertheless a somewhat mysterious figure in both local history and that of Hollywood. That she was born in Shreveport and that the family were communicants of St. Mark's Episcopal Church is definitely established. A short time after her birth, her parents separated, and she was taken in infancy by her mother, Lilly Pearl Miles Reilly, who later called herself Charlotte Shelby, to nearby Mansfield, where her maternal grandmother resided (her grandfather, Dr. Elmer Milton Miles, had been a pioneer surgeon of Sabine Parish and owned farmland in DeSoto). Juliet's father, Jason Homer Reilly, later returned to his native Dallas, Texas.

When she became a professional actress, Juliet was first called "Little Juliet Shelby" but was soon redubbed "Mary Miles Minter" to circumvent child labor laws. Mary Miles Minter was a real person's name, however—two, actually. The name had previously and legitimately belonged to two real relatives of young Juliet's. One was her aunt, her mother's sister, and the other was that same aunt's daughter. The aunt died in 1896 at the age of twenty-two and the cousin had died in 1903 at the age of eight. It was the identity of this cousin that Juliet Reilly assumed, creating controversy about her real age for decades to come.

The young girl with the stage name of her late cousin was not an actress by choice. She was talented, to be sure, but her rise to stardom came through the relentless efforts of her mother, an unsuccessful actress who pushed Juliet (and for a time did so with her other daughter, Margaret, as well) to achieve the fame that had eluded her. Ultimately, Juliet Reilly, as Mary Miles Minter, became the chief rival of Mary Pickford for "innocent girl" roles so popular in that day. Juliet, whom we shall refer to henceforth as Mary, once confided, "I never liked acting. My mother made me act. I never liked acting at all." Charlotte Shelby was, as one observer described her, "the quintessential stage mother."

In 1912, four years after her stage debut, Mary Miles Minter made her first film, *The Nurse*. At the same time, she was starring on Broadway in the hit play *The Littlest Rebel*, which ran from 1911 through 1914. In 1915, she went to Hollywood, where, over the next eight years, she made fifty-one more films, including 1919's *Anne of Green Gables*, which critics hailed as her finest work and one of the finest films of the era.

All copies of the version of *Anne of Green Gables* starring Minter (the first film version of the story ever made) are believed lost, and of her fifty-two films, only five are known to have survived: *The Eyes of the Deep* (1918), *The Ghost of Rose Taylor* (1918), *Nurse Marjorie* (1920), *A Cumberland Romance* (1920) and *The Little Clown* (1921).

Anne of Green Gables and three other films of Minter's were made under the direction of then famous Hollywood film director William Desmond Taylor. Taylor and Minter began an affair about this time, when she was seventeen and he nearly thirty years older. Some accounts suggest that the two became secretly engaged, but there is no evidence to support this. There is, however, evidence to support the fact that Taylor was bisexual and that Mary's infatuation with him was not reciprocated at the level of her own devotion to and pursuit of the romance.

In any event, the whole thing ended abruptly when, late on the night of February 1, 1922, Taylor was murdered in his home in the Westlake section of Los Angeles by an unknown assailant. His body was found, shot through the back, by Taylor's houseboy the next morning. Love letters from Minter, some in code written on her stationery, as well as love notes from the actress Mabel Normand (whose own career was similarly wrecked in 1930 by her involvement in the famous Fatty Arbuckle sex scandal) were found in the house, as well as some of Mary Miles Minter's monogrammed lingerie.

The murder became a national sensation almost instantaneously. Numerous suspects were questioned but the murder was never solved. Ellery Queen and Raymond Chandler, both detective writers, each fictionalized the case, and in 1967, film director King Vidor made a private investigation into the murder. In 1970, Rod Serling put together a documentary on the murder for CBS, in which Mary herself was implicated. Mary came out of seclusion afterward long enough to unsuccessfully sue Serling and CBS for slander. In 1986, a nonfiction treatment of the murder case based on the research of Vidor and entitled *A Cast of Killers*, by Sidney D. Kirkpatrick, was published. Nevertheless, to this day the killing of William Desmond Taylor remains an unsolved mystery.

Regardless, the career of Mary Miles Minter died, for all intents and purposes, with William Desmond Taylor. The chief suspect in the eyes of many was Charlotte Shelby, who saw Taylor as a threat to her daughter's career and had even sought a court order to keep the two apart. Charlotte was never prosecuted for the murder or, for lack of evidence, even arrested.

Suspicion hovered over her like a storm cloud for the rest of her life, however. It was speculated at the time by law enforcement authorities, journalists and others that Charlotte had dumped the murder weapon—which was never found—in Shreveport during a trip here immediately after the killing, though it was never proven one way or another if Charlotte in fact had anything to do with the murder. If Shelby did murder Taylor, her actions had the opposite effect from the one desired. In 1923, Minter made her last film and then parted ways with her mother, at least professionally.

In time, mother and daughter reconciled, though Mary never returned to acting. The two visited Shreveport and Mansfield several times before Shelby's death in 1957, but whether Mary ever visited her hometown again after that is uncertain.

Shortly after her mother's death, Mary, by then fifty-five years old, married a Los Angeles–area real estate agent named Brandon O'Hildebrandt. It was her first and only marriage, and in 1965, she was widowed. Sixteen years later, Mary Miles Minter was robbed of some $300,000 worth of jewelry and cash by thieves who broke into her Santa Monica home, beat her and left her for dead after she attempted to foil the robbery. She survived, however, and lived another three years in seclusion, dying of heart failure on August 5, 1984, at the age of eighty-two. Scant attention was paid to her passing, though *Variety* did do a short piece on her life and the *Los Angeles Times* published her obituary under the name she then used, Mary O'Hildebrandt. It indicated but little the fame she once had. Following a private funeral service in the Episcopal Church of St. Augustine by the Sea in Santa Monica, her remains were cremated and scattered in the Pacific Ocean. Only her legacy survives her, for she left no heirs.

In the Mansfield City Cemetery, there stands a twenty-one-foot-tall white marble obelisk inscribed "Sacred to the memory of Mary Miles Minter." It is not the actress's resting place, but rather that of her aunt and cousin, whose name she used. Indeed, it was erected and paid for by the actress Mary Miles Minter to honor those whose names she had used as her own. She, Juliet Reilly, a.k.a. Mary Miles Minter, sadly has no monument except a star on the Hollywood Walk of Stars on Vine Avenue in Los Angeles, a late tribute to her pioneering contributions to the film industry and to a career that ended tragically and all too soon.

BURCH AND BILL GRABILL, CHRONICLERS OF SHREVEPORT

It is no exaggeration to say that photographer William Grabill and his father, Burch Grabill, were the two outstanding chroniclers of Shreveport's twentieth-century growth and development. Additionally, they were preservers of historic photographs taken by nineteenth-century Shreveport photographers. In both respects, the Grabills, of Grabill Studios, contributed enormously to the documentation and preservation of old Shreveport, at least in images.

Grabill Studios got its start in Shreveport in 1919 when Burch E. Grabill, a native of Pennville, Indiana, came to Shreveport. A veteran of the Spanish-American War, Grabill had photographed the U.S. Army in action in the Philippines. In 1900, he became the official photographer for the University of Arkansas and settled in Fayetteville, where he met and, in 1903, married his wife, Maude A. Davis. The Grabills had two sons, Fletcher and William, before moving to Alexandria, Louisiana, in 1916, where he set up a private studio.

After only three years in Alexandria, the Grabills moved to Shreveport, where he set up his business doing portrait photography. Buying out the stocks of earlier photographers, several of which had begun operation in the nineteenth century, Grabill was able to preserve the negatives of many hundreds of images of the Shreveport area taken even before his arrival here.

His own work went far beyond portrait photography, capturing images of the life and culture of 1920s and 1930s Shreveport. With his son, Bill, who eventually became his business partner and, after his death in 1936, his successor, Burch Grabill also photographed many of Shreveport's streets and buildings and took numerous panoramic views of the city and the development of its downtown skyline.

Some of Shreveport's earliest aerial photographs were taken by Bill Grabill, who began flying at the age of sixteen and was still flying only months before his death at age eighty. At seventeen, he became the *only* photographer for the *Shreveport Journal* and continued in that role for a dozen years. During the 1930s, he also served as official photographer for Centenary College, much as his father had done for the University of Arkansas many years before. His flying experience led to his serving as an instructor to Army Air Corps pilots during World War II.

Burch (left) and Bill Grabill, who would later be his partner and successor in operating Grabill Studios of Shreveport. *Author's collection.*

Like his father before him, Bill Grabill continued to operate Grabill Studios as a portrait studio, though he much preferred the work of commercial aerial photography. He did a great deal of such work for area businesses, especially oil companies. Nevertheless, he found time to make numerous aerial shots of downtown Shreveport, Bossier City and developing parts of both. He also took many photographs chronicling the construction of major buildings and the evolution of the city's streets. Today, these photographs account for the vast majority of images used by historians and researchers to confirm or dispute facts for their texts.

For many years, Grabill Studios was located at 614 Milam Street but eventually moved to a refurbished house at the northeast corner of Kings Highway and Samford Avenue. When the construction of Interstate 49 through Shreveport began in the late 1980s, however, the familiar green building of Grabill Studios vanished along with so many other landmarks and memories. Grabill packed everything up, moved the large files of photographs and negatives to his garage apartment and retired.

Many of Grabill's photographs are now housed at the LSU-Shreveport Noel Memorial Library Archives. Some of these were used in the 1985 book *Shreveport: A Photographic Remembrance*, by LSUS archivist Pat Meador and *Shreveport Journal* editor Bailey Thompson. Many portraits of noted Shreveporters taken by both Burch and Bill Grabill were used in the 1931 *Shreveport Men and Women Builders*, by J. Ed Howe, and in the 1937 *History of Shreveport and Shreveport Builders* as well as its 1951 update of the same title, both by Howe and Lila McLure. Additionally, the Grabills captured on film numerous nationally noted personalities who passed through or performed in Shreveport. For years after Bill's death, the vast majority of the Grabill Studios' files remained packed up and unsorted, much as Bill Grabill left them at his death in January 1994. Fortunately, however, his heirs later saw fit to place the photos and negatives at the LSU-Shreveport Archives, the primary repository for early Shreveport and north Louisiana primary source data.

Although Grabill Studios has long vanished from the local scene, and although it has now been many years since Bill Grabill died, the legacy of the Grabills and of Grabill Studios will continue to live as long as there are people interested in studying and documenting the history of the Shreveport metropolitan area.

The Wiener Brothers, Architects of Enduring Innovations

Shreveport has a wealth of twentieth-century buildings, among which are a number of significant examples of the International style. Several Shreveporters were pioneers of this style, and among these the most notable were the brothers Samuel and William Wiener.

Sons of a prosperous grocer also named Samuel G. Wiener, Sam Wiener (1896–1977) and William Wiener Sr. (1907–1981) were young architects in the 1930s when the International and Moderne styles, which had reached their zenith in the 1920s in Europe, especially in Germany, began to be widely used in the South. Ironically, the Wiener brothers grew up in one of the city's most flamboyant Victorian mansions, the house that later was home to the Florentine Club, still standing in the 700 block of Austin Place. The style they would espouse, however, was one of stark lines and

Samuel G. Wiener Jr. *Author's collection.*

William B. Wiener Sr. *Author's collection.*

colors, of glass and steel construction in almost mechanical form; it was a total departure from the past and one that would have been unsettling, even shocking, to the eye at the time.

Working independently or more often together, the Wieners put Shreveport on the twentieth-century architectural map, as it were. In recent years, many of their surviving creations have been listed in the National Register of Historic Places because of their pioneering significance.

The Wiener brothers' most important works were the result of their architects' attempts to find and create a style appropriate to the modern spirit of the young century. Inspirations were the German Bauhaus School and such eminent yet radical architects of the day as Walter Gropius, Mies van der Rohe, Le Corbusier, Erich Mendelsohn, Alvar Aalto and Frank Lloyd Wright.

The Wieners (who also designed many notable area buildings in more traditional styles) visited with many of these architects, studied their works and were inspired by their designs. They did not, however, copy their work, but rather developed a new direction in Modernism using elements borrowed from their European colleagues but creating many innovations of their own. So innovative were they that their own works won accolades both in the United States and abroad, and in a relatively short time, the Wieners came to be ranked alongside many of their fellow Modernists in importance.

Among important Modernist buildings in Shreveport are the Wile house at 626 Wilder Place, designed by Sam Wiener in 1934 for grocer Ed Wile, who had to hire security guards to keep the curious from wandering, uninvited, into his home. Wile also employed the Wieners to design his grocery stores and adjacent shopping centers, including the Broadmoor Shopping Center on Youree and the Big Chain Shopping Center on Jewell at Lakeshore. The Broadmoor Big Chain store, with its sweeping ship's stern–like curved north face, is hailed internationally as the prototype of the modern supermarket. Closed in the 1970s, the Broadmoor Big Chain store later housed a furniture business but sadly burned in an early morning fire in 2003. The nearby Broadmoor Theatre, an integral but freestanding part of the Broadmoor Shopping Center and a much-loved Shreveport landmark, had been needlessly demolished almost two years earlier. Today, only a small fraction of the original Broadmoor Shopping Center remains standing, although the Jewella Shopping Center is largely intact.

Other Wiener-designed groceries for the Big Chain group (which was, incidentally, the successor to the Wiener-Loeb Grocery Company, operated by the Wiener brothers' father) include the 1920s Art Deco–style store on Fairfield now occupied by Harrison Paint Co. and other tenants; the starkly International-style Uptown Shopping Center, a 1950s complex that now bears little resemblance to its original appearance (likewise Heart O' Bossier in Bossier City, also built for the Big Chain Company); and the eclectic, almost Mediterranean-style Big Chain store that stood on Highland Avenue at Kings Highway from the 1930s through the 1960s. Demolished and replaced by a Safeway store, the site is now occupied by the Kings Highway Brookshire's.

Apart from the Wile house, important Wiener houses still standing include the Flesh-Walker house at 415 Sherwood Road, designed by William Wiener Sr. for geologist David Flesh in 1935 and now listed on the National register of Historic Places. William Wiener Sr. also designed the Charles Mayer house at 907 River Road (visible from East Kings Highway across the Old River duck pond) in 1938. Although altered, the Mayer house—once the center of the Shreve Island Plantation that covered the land now occupied by the Broadmoor Terrace and Broadmoor Annex subdivisions—still maintains its stark and sober Bauhaus appearance. Painted white, the rectangular house with its flat roof and louverlike windows almost resembles a gigantic beehive. Next door is the city's largest (but not only) round house, an unusual structure designed by a Wiener protégé but not by the Wiener brothers, as is often assumed.

Sam Wiener's own residence at 615 Longleaf Road was built in 1937, and although its original banded brickwork has been painted, the house is essentially unaltered. The Longleaf Road house is listed in the National Register of Historic Places today. After its completion in 1937, the Wieners held a party to hail its opening. Mrs. Wiener liked to quote a friend of hers who was overheard to comment that the house's design made it look like "a Coca-Cola factory." Nearby, on Longleaf Circle, a small cul-de-sac running off Longleaf Lane, are two nearly identical homes designed by William Wiener, one of them as his own residence. Today it is the Shreveport residence of his son, Bill Wiener Jr., also an architect and active historic preservation advocate.

At Cross Lake in 1933, the Wiener family built a weekend lake house that later became the residence of the Gerard family. Designed by William, it stood on the south shore of the lake, just off South Lakeshore Drive, but eventually fell into disuse and was demolished. Not far away and about the same time, the Wieners designed the El Karubah Shrine Clubhouse on Cross Lake. Though somewhat altered, it remains in use today.

Important commercial buildings include the Palomar Motel on Greenwood Road (1938), the Broadmoor Shopping Center (1940; largely destroyed by fire in 2003), the now demolished Broadmoor Theatre, the El Karubah Clubhouse on Cross Lake (1931) and several smaller but no less significant residences around the city, including the Coleman house at 123 Preston (1938; now listed on the National Register), the Herold house at 1050 Ontario (1947) and the notable modern house at 3145 Old Mooringsport Road (late 1930s).

Other significant structures by the Wiener brothers include the original State Fair Stadium (of which today's Independence Stadium is an expansion). It was Sam Wiener's first important work, designed when he was just starting out in his early twenties and working for the Shreveport firm of Jones, Roeselle and Olschner, in which he would later be a partner before forming his own firm.

Another early Samuel Wiener design is the Municipal Auditorium on Grand (now Elvis Presley) Avenue at Milam Street (1927–29), designed by Sam Wiener with fellow Shreveport architect Seymour Van Os and considered by many to be the state's premier example of Art Deco design. The old Feibelman Department Store Building (1925), on Texas Street at Louisiana downtown, later home to Sears and now vacant, was a notable early Sam Wiener design in the Neoclassical style.

More Bauhaus-influenced designs include the city incinerator on Kings Highway near Linwood (1935; now demolished), which won multiple architectural awards and was featured even in European architecture journals of the 1930s as *the* model of its type; the Orthopedic Clinic (later the Children's Clinic) on Line Avenue at Margaret Place (1936; now demolished); the old Downtown Airport (1931; now demolished); the old Municipal Airport (1952; now the TAC Air terminal on the Regional Airport site); as well as several area schools, including Bossier and Haughton High Schools, Werner Park Elementary School and Broadmoor and Linwood Junior High Schools, to name but a few.

Sam Wiener also was the local consulting architect working with the New York City firm of McKim, Mead and White on the design of the Commercial National Bank Building at Texas and Edwards Streets, completed in 1940. In 1950, together with local architects William C. Gilmer and J.P. Annan, he designed the Mid-City Motor Hotel and adjoining East Building of Physicians and Surgeons Hospital, located at the southeast corner of Jordan Street and Line Avenue. Not an especially aesthetically pleasing complex, the structure is nevertheless massive and innovative in many respects. Its large central courtyard allows all of the rooms in the huge complex to receive natural light, and all the windows are sheltered by a unique system of ledgelike streamlined steel awnings. At one time, the building was connected to the other structures in the Physicians and Surgeons Hospital by means of an enclosed pedestrian bridge over Line Avenue. This interesting feature was unfortunately removed in the late 1990s when Christus-Schumpert Medical Center acquired Physicians and Surgeons and demolished the portion of its complex west of Line Avenue.

Shreve City Shopping Center, built in the early 1960s, was designed by William Wiener Sr. and his son, Bill Jr., and though considerably altered in design, it is still largely intact in form. Shreve City was the area's first large "strip" shopping center, designed around its parking lots and incorporating multiple but interconnected structures differing in scale and massing. Other structures within the parking lot broke the stark continuity of the design. The round building, the partially glass-skinned bank, the flaring roofs over the covered parking lot islands (now altered) and the (now removed) round mushroomlike shelters with their tall stemlike columns tapering out as they reached the roof were all innovative touches that grew directly out of the Wieners' earlier International-style works. Also drawing from the Wiener tradition is the old Commercial National Bank's former Motor Bank, located at the southwest corner of Milam and Market Streets. With its wavy lines, open spaces and use of glass, tile and structural steel, this Bill Wiener Jr. design of the 1970s is reminiscent of the innovative works of his father and uncle forty years earlier.

The International and related Modernist styles had a profound effect on later twentieth-century architectural design and building techniques. Shreveport can be justly proud to have the exceptional collection of early examples that it does and to have been home to Sam and William Wiener, two important pioneers of the genre in the United States.

JANET CURRIE, BEAUTY QUEEN AND ACTRESS

Considered a great beauty in her day but now all but forgotten from the history of stage and screen, actress and Shreveport native Janet Currie seemed destined for stardom when she died suddenly at the age of twenty-five. Born in 1909, her grandfather was former mayor Andrew Currie, who, up until Clyde Fant became mayor in 1946, held the record for longest-serving chief executive officer of the city (twelve years). A city park memorializes Mayor Currie today. Janet's great-uncle, the notorious Texas lawman and sometime outlaw James "Big Jim" Currie, is best remembered for attempting to kill actor Maurice Barrymore in nearby Marshall, Texas, in 1881.

One of four children, Janet had a brother, Andrew Currie III, and two sisters, Mary Bell and Adeline. The children grew up in their grandparents' home at 826 Spring Street, a grand old Gothic Revival Victorian mansion that had once been the residence of local druggist T.H. Morris, whose firm, Morris & Dickson, still operates today (the house still stands too, though now shorn of much of its gingerbread and

Janet Currie. *Author's collection.*

long ago moved to Lake Bistineau by the Beene family of Bossier Parish to be a lake house).

Janet's father was in the auto business and her grandfather, the former mayor, was in real estate. Later, the family moved to 502 Jordan Street, where her mother lived even after Janet's untimely death.

At the age of eighteen, a recent graduate of Byrd High School, Janet Currie was selected "Miss Shreveport." That was in 1928, and it was through this pageant that she was "discovered." The legendary showman Earl Carroll, of the Earl Carroll Follies, a New York–based vaudeville revue that featured beautiful young women and was charged with a high degree of sexuality for the era, hired Janet and two other Shreveport girls from the pageant, Diana White and Catherine Griggs O'Neill, for his *Sketchbook Revue*. Janet alone received a three-year contract from Carroll, however. In 1930, Earl Carroll said of Janet Currie that "even in a bevy of stunning beauties this fair charmer stands out." She was then the star of the *Sketchbook Revue*, running at the Forty-fourth Street Theatre in New York City.

The *Police Gazette*, a moderately salacious periodical of the time, chose Janet as "the crowning queen of them all" among the vaudeville beauties of Gotham in 1930 and pictured her in a see-through dress—very shocking for the era, despite the high Art Deco styling of the garment. The statuesque Miss Currie and the cut of the gown, such as it was, are reminiscent of Erté, the great Art Deco artist, who was in his prime at the time. Said the *Gazette:* "[Her] face and form are glamorous and, besides, Janet has an abundance of 'It.'"

Later in 1930, Janet withdrew from her contract with Carroll and moved to Hollywood, where she had a small part in a movie called *Flying High* and another in the original version of *Sidewalks of New York.*

She didn't remain long in Hollywood, though, for on a visit home to Shreveport at Christmas 1931, shortly after *Sidewalks of New York* was released, she eloped with one Ben James, vowing to quit acting and settle down to domestic life. The couple honeymooned in Chicago, resided briefly in Kansas City and then even more briefly with Ben's family at 260 Robinson Place. By the end of 1932, the Jameses were separated and Janet had filed for divorce.

With the divorce pending, Janet returned to California and acting. There she entered into a contract with MGM, starring in several modest films before doing a stint with the Three Stooges, beginning with 1932's *Meet the Baron.*

Although her movies and her roles in them were generally not memorable, Janet was successful in Hollywood and continued to work on a regular basis. Her looks attracted the young glamour photographer George Hurrell, who photographed her both for the studios and as a subject of his own artistry. Though Hurrell was only starting out at the time, he later would become Hollywood's top photographer and, arguably, for a time the world's foremost glamour photographer. His early images of Janet Currie feature his trademark use of contrasting light and shadow, made all the more pronounced by the black-and-white images.

In any event, just as her career was taking off and her roles improving, just as she was becoming a glamour icon and appearing regularly in film magazines and glamour and fashion layouts, Janet Currie's career suddenly came to an end.

On December 21, 1934, Janet Currie died in her Hollywood home. Her obituaries make no mention of the cause of death beyond simply "a long illness." One is left to wonder what that illness was that would have claimed the life of a rising twenty-five-year-old actress and glamour queen who only a few months previously—so the illness could not have been that long-lived in truth—was cutting up with the Three Stooges, posing for George Hurrell and appearing in *Photoplay*.

Her parents, siblings and both grandmothers survived her. Her funeral was held quietly in Shreveport and her name all but vanished from the annals of Hollywood.

So what are the missing pieces of this story? The standard references—and even the obscure ones—on Hollywood and vaudeville give no clues. She is absent from Internet sources on cinema and theatre history; she is barely found referenced anywhere, yet she attained a degree of importance and certainly of a brand of titillating notoriety. How did she die and from what causes, what became of Ben James and what were the circumstances of their short marriage and sudden divorce?

Few are living today who would have known Janet Currie personally, though some may be. In any case, the life and too early death of this beautiful Shreveport-born actress who might well have gone on to become a Hollywood icon, had she lived but a bit longer, remain a curious historical enigma.

Maestro Fausto Magnani

Among the many tens of thousands of tombstones of Forest Park Cemetery can be found a small black granite monument reading "Here sleeps Maestro Fausto Magnani." What a name that is! And Maestro? What did he conduct? Who might he have been? How did he come to be buried in Shreveport? Here is the Maestro's tale.

Fausto Magnani (pronounced "mun-yany") was born in Nice, France, on February 26, 1899, the son of Italian parents. He lived a somewhat bohemian existence in his youth, spending time in Paris, Genoa and along the Riviera. He was thoroughly a European of the generation that came of age before the First World War. Fascinated by music, he trained as a cellist and later became an orchestral conductor.

Magnani was a pupil of the conductor Arthur Nikisch and was principal cellist under Toscanini at La Scala, Milan's great theatre, once

Fausto Magnani. *Author's collection.*

the domain of Verdi. He was also a composer, though he published little prior to 1935. His catalogue of compositions includes two operas in English, one symphony, numerous dances and impressionist pieces, adaptations of Italian songs and compositions for the violin, viola and violincello.

Mrs. Fausto Magnani was an interesting character in her own right. Born Josephine Margaret Cunningham in Chicago in 1888, she eloped with Milton W. Kirk, the son of soap and perfume baron James S. Kirk of Chicago, when she was only fourteen and he in his thirties. Kirk died in 1915, leaving Mollie, as she was known, a widow at twenty-seven. He also left her $1 million in trust, from which she was paid an income for the duration of her life.

Mollie, who never had children, traveled the world during the 1920s and '30s. In Europe, she met Fausto, who spent as much of his time as possible on the Riviera, especially in Biarritz. In 1936, the two married and came to America, where they lived happily on Mollie's first husband's income and where Fausto seems to have remained in an almost constant state of contention with the IRS. Eventually he became a U.S. citizen, though he did little composing or playing the cello anymore.

Interestingly enough, however, after coming to America Fausto did begin to conduct more frequently, especially (though rather ironically) in Europe. In late 1949, he led the Orchestra Sinfonica di Roma in a concert series broadcast across Italy over Radio della Italia. In 1951, he was guest conductor of the Vienna Symphony and the Pasdeloup Orchestra in France, as well as orchestras in Lisbon, Portugal, and Genoa, Italy, where his mother resided. He also was guest conductor at La Scala on at least one occasion.

In 1948, Fausto conducted two "gala concerts" in Los Angeles's Wilshire Ebell Theatre. The program for these performances included a brief biography written by Magnani himself, which placed him among "the first rank of the world's greatest conductors," a humble self-analysis, to say the least.

A reviewer for the *Los Angeles Times* described Magnani's conducting style as suggestive of "an operatic background—the presumably dramatic overlong pauses, the great show of cuing, the whipping up of climaxes to a pitch of fury, and various histrionic indulgences which often gave the impression of a wild animal restricted by the bars of too small a cage." He went on to describe one piece as "mainly providing an opportunity for the unrestrained exercise of conductorial gymnastics, with Tchaikovsky belatedly bringing up the rear."

The Magnanis resided at Santa Barbara, California's luxurious Hotel Mirasol, where they lived up until Mollie's death in 1958. Some years earlier, they had met prominent Shreveport lawyer C. Huffman Lewis and his wife Jen, who regularly summered in Santa Barbara. After Mollie's death, the Lewises persuaded Fausto to move to Shreveport, and in 1964 he did, first residing at 4003 Baltimore and then at 591 Oneonta. As he grew older, Magnani's imagination grew more fertile and detached from reality. By the time of his death, for example, he was convinced that he was actually the illegitimate son of the last czarina of Russia.

Magnani never conducted the Shreveport Symphony, except as a guest, nor did he seek to become especially active in the city's musical circles, beyond the society aspects of these. He did once make an ill-conceived proposal to conduct the Dallas Symphony, though it came to naught. Despite not being especially active musically during his life in Shreveport, he insisted on being called "Maestro" and was even listed in the city directory as such. On February 23, 1980, three days before his eighty-first birthday, Maestro Magnani died in Shreveport.

He was buried at Forest Park Cemetery on his birthday. His friend and attorney Arthur R. Carmody Jr., a partner in the firm that Huffman Lewis had been with for many years, saw to it that his grave was marked properly. Sadly, however, another artist of note, the sculptor Arthur Morgan, whose works are to be found in such hallowed venues as Statuary Hall in the U.S. Capitol Building and who died in 1994, is buried only fifteen lots to the west of Magnani in an unmarked grave beside the elegant monument he created for his daughter, who died in a fire as a child. Both artists' graves are on the north side of the southernmost road of Forest Park Cemetery, just west of the intersection of the north-running road, midway between the St. Vincent and Linwood Avenue boundaries of the cemetery.

JEAN DESPUJOLS, ARTIST

The Meadows Museum on the Centenary College campus is home to the well-known collection of Indochina paintings by the French American artist Jean Despujols. Less well known, however, is the artist himself, although his was a rich and important career in which Shreveport played a significant role, Conversely, he played a significant role in Shreveport.

Jean Despujols (pronounced "day-poo-joe") was born on March 19, 1886, in Salles, France. He attended the Lycée de Bordeaux and then the Municipal School of Fine Arts, where he studied under Paul Quinsac, who encouraged him to pursue further studies at the École Nationale des Beaux-Arts in Paris.

His studies and the beginning of his career were interrupted by the First World War. For four years, from 1914 to 1918, Despujols was a machine gunner in the trenches, seeing action at Verdun, the Chemin des Dames, the Belgian Campaign and the Marne. During this time, the young artist produced numerous moving and graphic sketches of both the carnage and the life of the soldiers during the "war to end all wars."

After the war, Despujols went to Rome, advancing his career further. There he met the director of the Fontainebleau School of Fine Arts, who hired him as a professor at the school. During the remainder of the 1920s up through 1936, Despujols experienced his most creative period. He exhibited at France's most celebrated salons and galleries and was much acclaimed. His extraordinary nudes were produced during this time,

Jean Despujols (right) modeling for a bust by sculptor Arthur C. Morgan (left) of Shreveport, circa 1960. *Photograph by Langston McEachern. Author's collection.*

including his own favorite painting, *Naissance de Venus*. Among techniques Despujols developed during this period were painting in wax and the use of twenty-four-karat gold to highlight his canvases.

In the volatile thirties, Despujols became interested in politics. He was essentially independent, however, and was disliked both by the radical right and the radical left. Eventually, he decided it would be wise to leave Europe, traveling to French Indochina under the auspices of the Society of Colonial Artists and the Grand Economic Council of France. There he spent twenty months creating some 360 paintings. In 1939, he returned to France, but the outbreak of war caused him again to leave his country, this time permanently.

Despujols came to the United States, joining his American-born wife and their children, who had left ahead of him. Initially residing in Minneapolis, the family came to Shreveport in 1941 at the invitation of a former student, Theo Minge Randall, a Shreveport native who later played a considerable role in the arts in New Mexico. Mrs. Randall suggested Shreveport because of its excellent opportunities at the time, having an oil- and gas-based economy with many well-to-do potential customers for portraits; she was right.

In Shreveport, Despujols created portraits for dozens of families. The works depict many of the social, civic and mercantile leaders of the city during the 1940s, 1950s and early 1960s. Most are in private collections, but two exhibits of Despujols' portraiture have been displayed by the Meadows Museum, first in 1978 and another in 1996.

But Jean Despujols did not create only portraits during his residence here. He also created an extraordinary series of paintings with deep and powerful social themes. These, called the "taboo collection," were painted under the pseudonym "Janjol" and reflect the artist's political and societal vision of the world. These paintings have never been exhibited in a public showing; hopefully that will one day change. They are privately held in Shreveport, but a few images from this series were reproduced for the first time in the autumn 1996 issue of *Louisiana Cultural Vistas*, the quarterly journal of the Louisiana Endowment for the Humanities.

Despujols died in Shreveport on January 26, 1965, and was buried at Greenwood Cemetery on Stoner Avenue. On his gravestone are listed his many awards: the Prix de la Ville, the Medaille d'or de Paris, the Premier Grand Prix de Rome de Peinteur, the Prix de L'Indochine, the Croix de Guerre avec six citations, the Medaille Militaire and the Legion d'Honneur.

The Indochina collection was hidden by Despujols at his family home in Bordeaux throughout World War II; in 1948, he had it shipped to Shreveport. A portion of the collection was reproduced in the April 1951 issue of the *National Geographic Magazine*, as well as a photograph of Despujols unloading his paintings after their arrival here.

Except for brief showings at the Smithsonian in 1950 and the Louisiana State Exhibit Building soon thereafter, the Despujols Indochina paintings remained crated at his 503 Broadmoor Boulevard home for years after their arrival here. In 1969, the collection was purchased intact, per the artist's wish, by oil operator Algur H. Meadows, who in 1974 made provisions for the old Centenary College Administration Building to be remodeled into a museum to properly house them. Thus was born the Meadows Museum, and thus does Jean Despujols continue to live and speak to us even four and a half decades after his death.

W. Zolley Lerner, a.k.a. Film Director Thomas Z. Loring

Years ago there lived in Shreveport a veteran of the motion picture industry named W. Zolley Lerner. Most of his friends and associates knew him as an oil company executive who had a keen interest in the Shreveport Little Theater and the Marjorie Lyons Playhouse at Centenary, both of which were organizations with which he was deeply involved. Few realized his importance to the history of the movie industry.

Zolley Lerner was born in Warsaw, Poland, on March 17, 1908, and as a child of four immigrated to the United States with his parents. He grew up in Kansas City, Missouri, and was educated at the University of Nebraska, from which he graduated in 1929. In 1932, he received his master's degree from the same institution and then served on the faculty in the drama department.

Lerner was regarded as an authority on the history structure of the traditional Eastern European Jewish dramatic style known as the Yiddish theatre and wrote extensively on the subject. He also wrote several plays during this time, including a popular comedy entitled *These Four Years* (1937), and was founding director of Kansas City's famous Resident Theatre for eight before leaving for a directing job with Twentieth Century Fox in Los Angeles in 1940.

In Hollywood, Lerner directed several motion pictures under the name Thomas Z. Loring. Among his most notable films are *Through Different Eyes* (1942); *Who Is Hope Schuylar?* (1942), a dramatization of the Pulitzer Prize–winning novel *Hearses Don't Hurry*; *He Hired the Boss* (1943); and *They Came to Blow Up America* (1943).

In 1944 and 1945, Lerner worked as a filmmaker for the U.S. Army, working under Frank Capra. It was during this period that he made the classic documentary *Ernie Pyle's New Mexico*. He also produced and shot newsreels for the U.S. Army in Germany for official release.

Following the end of the war, Lerner returned to civilian moviemaking as a test director for Twentieth Century Fox. It was there that he gave a young actress named Norma Jean Baker her first film tests in 1946. Norma Jean, of course, would later go on to fame under the name Marilyn Monroe; Lerner is credited with being her "discoverer."

During this same period, Lerner, as Loring, directed several more feature films, including *My Dream Is Yours* (1949), starring Doris Day. In all, Lerner worked on productions with Fox, Universal, Warner and Columbia Studios during the period from 1940 to 1950, in addition to his army tenure and his independent film work. In 1950, he returned to stage directing, working on theatrical productions in Los Angeles and New York, off-Broadway. He left the entertainment industry in 1954 to enter the oil and gas business, relocating to Shreveport, where he established the Ko-Ler Oil Company, whose office was located in the Johnson Building on Milam Street.

In Shreveport, Lerner continued, on occasion, to direct stage plays, and for many years he and his wife, Leah, attended virtually every theatre, symphony and opera performance that took place in Shreveport of Bossier City.

Leah Lerner's health took a dramatic turn for the worse in June 1964 when she suffered a near-fatal stroke while she and Zolley were vacationing in Philadelphia. After awakening from a month-long coma, Leah spent the next seven years recuperating, with Zolley's help. Physical therapy and rehabilitation were a long and arduous process for Leah, but she found an able nurse and caregiver in Zolley, who spent the years of recuperation taking his wife to Houston and Los Angeles for treatments not then available in Shreveport. Leah's health was never good again, even after her recovery, and she spent much of her time painting in a studio Zolley built for her in the couple's East Ridge Drive home. When Leah was well enough, the Lerners would again attend local theatre and symphony performances, becoming a familiar sight to other patrons with Zolley pushing Leah's wheelchair down the steep aisles to the very front of the theatre.

Even then, Zolley would sometimes find the time to direct a play or two, including what may have been the first examples of traditional Yiddish theatre seen on stage in Shreveport. His 1975 Shreveport Little Theater adaptation of the Yiddish classic *The Dybbuk* was met with particularly high critical praise. In addition to working with local theatre organizations, Zolley Lerner also served on the board of the Shreveport Symphony for many years, beginning in 1958, and was a member of the Shreveport Summer Theater board. Separately, Lerner was largely responsible for the revival of opera in Shreveport, directing the first opera productions for what ultimately would become the Shreveport Civic Opera.

In addition to his other contributions to local theatre, Lerner also worked with the Caddo Parish School System to bring live theatre to schoolchildren as an educational experience and to bring stage productions to underprivileged neighborhoods where—because of economics, transportation and cultural bias—residents might not otherwise have had the opportunity to experience them. He also volunteered occasionally as an instructor in drama at Centenary and LSUS.

Active to the end, Zolley Lerner died on July 11, 1986. Leah had died eight months earlier, and Zolley's health, fine until her death, began to deteriorate after losing her. The Lerners are buried at Mount Carmel Cemetery in the Kansas City, Missouri suburb of Raytown. They left two children—a son, James, and daughter, Amy. Although Zolley Lerner's ashes rest elsewhere and his children reside elsewhere, his contributions to Shreveport, his adopted home, will always be part of the city's legacy.